# ASYMMETRICAL

## BRIDGING THE GAP BETWEEN SCIENCE & HUMAN EXPERIENCE

Jonathan Chapman

# ASYMMETRICAL

## BRIDGING THE GAP BETWEEN SCIENCE & HUMAN EXPERIENCE

First published in Great Britain as a softback original in 2019

Copyright © Jonathan Chapman

www.asymmetricalbook.com

The moral right of this author has been asserted.

All rights reserved.

No part of this publication may be reproduced, stored in a retrieval system, or transmitted, in any form or by any means, without the prior permission in writing of the publisher, nor be otherwise circulated in any form of binding or cover other than that in which it is published and without a similar condition including this condition being imposed on the subsequent purchaser.

Typeset in Minion Pro

Editing, design, typesetting and publishing by UK Book Publishing

www.ukbookpublishing.com

ISBN: 978-1-913179-07-6

*To Fran*

It thus being settled that our question really aims at the ratio of two lengths – that of our body and that of the atom – with an incontestable priority of independent existence on the side of the atom, the question truly reads: Why must our bodies be so large compared with the atom?

Erwin Schrödinger, *What Is Life?*

A fact that most physicists still find somewhat staggering, a most profound and beautiful thing, is that, in quantum mechanics, *for each of the rules of symmetry there is a corresponding conservation law;* there is a definite connection between the laws of conservation and the symmetries of physical laws.

Richard Feynman, *Lectures on Physics*

# CONTENTS

1. **Introduction**     1
   The possibilities you see in the mirror     1
   Shearing layers     6
   Systems thinking     10

2. **The Idea Is Crystalline, the Fact Fluid**     15
   Systems, populations, objects & stuff     15
   The indeterminacy of identity     23
   Populations and types     28
   Maps and analogues     35
   Labelling the maps     40
   A theory is just a model     52

3. **Asymmetry and Scale**     63
   The physicists' argument     63
   The scientific picture     68
   Statistical and mechanical order     84
   The biologists' argument     92
   Constraints-oriented explanations     102
   Science and secularism     125

## 4. Authentic Intelligence — 131
- The imitation game — 131
- The persistence of meaning — 139
- In search of significance — 145
- Engineering intelligence — 152
- Introspection and consciousness — 161
- Intelligence and cultural performances — 168

## 5. Action and Practical Reasoning — 176
- Objectives, strategies and constraints — 176
- The heuristics of practical reasoning — 185
- Intention, process and outcomes — 199
- The problem of means and ends — 208
- Moral reasoning — 216
- What are we arguing about? — 227

## 6. Conclusion: Springing the Object Method Trap — 234

## Reference — 238
- List of Sources — 238

## Acknowledgements — 240

## Index — 241

CHAPTER ONE

# INTRODUCTION

### The possibilities you see in the mirror

Towards the beginning of his *Lectures on Physics*, Richard Feynman writes:

> *Everything is made of atoms. That is the key hypothesis. The most important hypothesis in all of biology, for example, is that everything that animals do, atoms do. In other words, there is nothing that living things do that cannot be understood from the point of view that they are made of atoms acting according to the laws of physics.*

But what does *'acting according to'* mean. My guess is that many science students and more than a few non-specialist readers will interpret this to mean biological events are determined by atoms acting according to the laws of physics. However, there is no justification for this interpretation. The most we can say is that all biological events are constrained by the properties of the atoms that compose biological entities.

Feynman suggests as an analogy that scientists investigating nature are like observers watching a game and trying to work out what the rules are. But to understand a game you need to know not only what the rules are but also what the purpose of the game is, who is playing and what the possibilities of the game are. The rules of the game constrain the possibilities but they don't determine them.

This is probably what Feynman intended, because a few lines later he says:

> *If instead of arranging the atoms in some definite pattern, again and again repeated, on and on, or even forming little lumps of complexity like the odor of violets, we make an arrangement which is always different from place to place, with different kinds of atoms arranged in many ways, continually changing, not repeating, how much more marvelously is it possible that this thing might behave? Is it possible that that 'thing' walking back and forth in front of you, talking to you, is a great glob of these atoms in a very complex arrangement, such that the sheer complexity of it staggers the imagination as to what it can do? When we say we are a pile of atoms, we do not mean we are merely a pile of atoms, because a pile of atoms which is not repeated from one to the other might well have the possibilities which you see before you in the mirror.*

'Not merely', though, remains vague. The problem is that our understanding of explanation in the sciences tends to be process-focused. Since the 18th century the default understanding of what it means to explain something scientifically has been structured in terms of the pattern of succession of cause and effect. The constraints within which a system evolves are treated as background conditions. However, any attempt to integrate physics with biology, and the scientific picture with a wider understanding, will require a multi-layered model of explanation and a multi-layered model will necessarily be constraints-oriented. Unfortunately, culturally and philosophically, we lack the concepts to make sense of constraints-oriented explanations.

In some ways this is odd, because that is the direction in which scientific practice has evolved. Scientific theorising in practice today means building and applying abstract conceptual models. This is how Stephen Hawking describes it in *A Brief History of Time*:

> *A theory is just a model of the universe...and a set of rules that relate quantities in the model to observations that we make. A theory is a good theory if it satisfies two requirements: it must accurately describe a large class of observations on the basis of a model that contains only a few arbitrary elements, and it must make definite predictions about the results of future observations.*

To this way of thinking there is still a set of rules but the rules are features of the model and not attributes of the natural world. A model maps more or less successfully to a domain of application. Because theoretical models are by their nature abstractions, and multiple abstractions can be applied to the same domain of observable reality, this approach doesn't impose a single layer of explanation on reality or insist that the rules in the model are in some way the rules in nature.

A conceptual framework that accommodates just the natural sciences isn't going to be enough to support an understanding of all the possibilities that we see in the mirror. To achieve that, the framework also has to extend to introspective experience and the idea of an ethical life.

The obstacle here is that in the wider cultural domain there is an equivalent problem concerning our ideas about language. Just as traditionally scientists thought they were discovering rules in nature, we typically think that words apply to objects – we suppose *words mean things*. But words are abstractions and therefore can only apply to the actual world through the application of conceptual models. We don't usually recognise this because language use is so intuitive. But the models do exist and technology is driving their excavation. Because computers have no capacity for intuitive understanding, software engineers, in order to build computer applications, have to make these intuitions about the target domain explicit, and when this happens the underlying conceptual models come into view.

As things stand, our image of the cosmos is fragmented and we lack the tools to make it cohere. We aren't able to connect the scientific picture of the world with our experience of existence as human beings. We can't explain how things hang together and we can't explain how they may not. Our understanding is composed of curiously disconnected islands of insight. This is a philosophical problem, a cultural problem and a personal problem.

I believe it is possible to build a single conceptual framework of explanation that reaches all the way from particle physics to ethical accountability. It should be emphasised, though, that any such schema is going to be very abstract. It will be a model of a model. Like algebra and logic, it will have global applicability only because it doesn't determine the substantive content of the model. That is its advantage. The purpose of the proposal is to create an opening to a possibility that at the moment is closed off, namely, an understanding of the world through multiple layers of explanation within a single conceptual framework.

# Shearing layers

Stewart Brand's *How Buildings Learn* is one of my favourite books. It is a book about buildings, and specifically how buildings are modified and adapted over time in a way that suggests they can be conceived as systems in time as well as systems in space. To illustrate his argument Brand uses sequences of photographs of the same building or street scene taken at different times, sometimes over many decades. The cover of my edition features two townhouses on a street in New Orleans, identical in an auctioneers drawing made in 1857, quite different in a 1993 photograph after various modifications to add storeys, extensions, balconies, windows and entrances.

The underlying insight is that although many buildings are designed and managed as spatial wholes, none are designed and managed as temporal wholes. There are very few theorists of building through time. Brand quotes the architect Frank Duffy to express the fundamental idea:

> Our basic argument is that there isn't such a thing as a building. A building properly conceived is several layers of longevity of built components. The unit of analysis for us isn't the building; it's the use of the building through time.

In his original article Duffy called these layers of longevity shearing layers. He distinguished four: the shell, the services, the space plan and the set. Brand extends and generalises this schema by adding the site and splitting the shell into structure and skin. This generates a six-layer schema for a building: the site, the structure, the skin, the services, the space plan and the set.

The site is the location; it is the geographical setting and the legally defined plot. The structure is the foundations and the load-bearing components. The skin is the exterior surfaces and the weatherproofing. The services are the conduits, cables, plumbing, channels for communication, monitoring, heating, ventilation, air conditioning and so on. The space plan is the interior layout and the way in which the space is partitioned to allow for circulation and use, and the set is all the stuff inside the building, such as the furniture and the appliances.

Each shearing layer operates to a different timescale. The site is more or less permanent from a human perspective. The structure should last at least 60 years, but in some cases may endure for several centuries. The exterior surfaces need to be replaced every 30 years or so and the services probably become outdated in 15. The partitioning is changed every few years, and the stuff is constantly being moved around and replaced. This layering also defines how the building relates to people. The individual occupant is concerned about the stuff, the tenant about the space plan, the owner about the services, the neighbours about the exterior surfaces and the community about the footprint and the usage of the site.

Function perpetually modifies form. As buildings are adapted over time to suit the needs of the occupants their form undergoes continuous modification. The sequences of photographs in

Brand's book demonstrate this continual flow, modification and transformation. This isn't quite the same idea as form follows function. Brand suggests that the founding idea of modernism as it was articulated by the high-rise architect Louis Sullivan in 1896 – *'form ever follows function'* – was misleading because it was static and missed the way that function changes through time.

The concept of shearing layers captures the idea that there is a potentially disruptive slippage between the fast-changing and the slow-changing components of a building. Because the layers are not insulated from each other, the longevity of a building is often determined by how well it can absorb new uses and new services technology. Brand's argument is that buildings can be built to be more adaptable.

> *An adaptive building has to allow slippage between the differently paced systems of Site, Structure, Skin, Services, Space Plan and Stuff. Otherwise the slow systems block the flow of the quick ones, and the quick ones tear up the slow ones within their constant change.*

The concept of shearing layers can be applied to other types of system in which the components change at different paces. The model can be applied with little adjustment to software systems, for example. When we talk about the architecture of a software system, it is not a metaphor. Similarly, ecosystems can be understood by observing the rates of change of different components.

> *Hummingbirds and flowers are quick, redwood trees slow, and whole redwood forests even slower. Most interaction is within the same pace level – hummingbirds and flowers pay attention to each other, oblivious to redwoods, who are oblivious to them. Meanwhile the forest is attentive to climate change, but not to the hasty fate of single trees. The insight is this: 'The dynamics of the system will be dominated by the slow components, with the rapid components simply following along'. Slow constrains quick; slow controls quick.*

Brand argues that adaptation isn't just a necessary response to an unavoidable problem. In building, as in nature, it is only through adaptation and accommodation that the possibility of harmony in systems can be achieved. He quotes the design theorist Christopher Alexander.

> *Things that are good have a certain kind of structure... You can't get that structure except dynamically... In nature you've got very-small-feedback-loop adaptation going on, which is why things get to be harmonious. That's why they have the qualities that we value. If it wasn't for the time dimension, it wouldn't happen.*

Not all change is adaptation. Growth is independent of adaptation, and constant churn, which Brand calls 'graceless turnover', can defeat it. Adaptation requires time and care and reciprocity.

# Systems thinking

This is a way of thinking that picks out systems within systems as the units of analysis. The concept of systems thinking is not new. It was developed in the 20th century to address some of the limitations of the analytical approach to understanding. This is how Paul Cilliers puts it in his book *Complexity & Postmodernism*:

> *One of the most important scientific tools has always been the analytical method. If something is too complex to be grasped as a whole, it is divided into manageable units which can be analysed separately and then put together again. However, the study of complex dynamic systems has uncovered a fundamental flaw in the analytical method. A complex system is not constituted merely by the sum of its components but also by the intricate relationships between these components. In 'cutting up' a system, the analytical method destroys what it seeks to understand.*

Systems thinking is concerned with building the conceptual toolkit necessary to understand complexity and the patterns of interaction in complex systems: non-linear interactions, feedback loops, framing, self-organisation and so on. In parallel, increases in computing capability have made it possible to run simulations that model the behaviour of complex systems and the way that they evolve. However, to the extent that it retains an underlying sense that the components of a complex system form an integrated whole, systems thinking tends to remain within the same paradigm as analytical thinking.

I call this paradigm 'compositionalism'. The basic idea is that things can be thought of in terms of parts and wholes. The polarities in compositional thinking are reductivism, which privileges the component parts, and essentialism, which privileges the whole. I don't think anyone has found either a satisfactory way to integrate these perspectives or offer an insight into the basis of the discontinuity.

A shear is a rupture created by strain in a structure. Shearing layers can be created by differences in the pace of change and differences in scale driven by differing dynamics. A shearing layer creates a discontinuity in a system, a layer of incommensurability. It refers to the fault-lines and the fractures in the integrity of systems. This applies both to conceptual systems and actual systems. Thomas Kuhn's model of revolutionary science as the transition from one paradigm to another across a layer of incommensurability can be seen as a description of the opening up of a shearing layer in a conceptual system.

These fault-lines and fractures aren't simply between different components of a single whole. Systems aren't necessarily stacked hierarchically, they typically intersect and overlap. For example, if we think about a building, the power supply, the water supply and the telecommunications are usually delivered through connections to the grid. In this respect the building can be viewed as the housing for some of the nodes on these networks. The grid systems intersect with the building, and through these connections, disruption created by the pace of change in the network gets transmitted to the building. Perhaps less obviously, the structure intersects with the terrain through the foundations, the skin intersects with the climate through the weatherproofing, and the space plan is a region within the wider organisation of partitioning and circulation that extends beyond the building into the outside environment, joining the interior to the exterior.

Analysed in this way, as the intersection of multiple systems, a building ceases to be either an integrated whole or a collection of component parts. This suggests a possible alternative to the paradigm of compositionalism and therefore a path to a way of thinking that avoids the polarities of reductivism and essentialism. This way of thinking supports an image of the world that is not only many-layered, indeterminate and open-ended but also loosely integrated, and therefore one where adjustment, accommodation and adaptation are the primary dynamics.

In order to bring this image into focus we need to re-examine our models of composition. My view is that compositionalism is more than just a pattern of thinking, a strategy, reductive or holistic, which we adopt in order to try to understand the world. I think it is also the consequence of a mistake built into how we form concepts and use language, a mistake that Wittgenstein called the idea that *'words mean things'*. For this reason, we need to re-examine our ideas about concept formation and the use of language.

What are the implications if *things* are conceptual structures that are imposed on the observable world rather than entities that actually exist? What does it mean if, instead, systems, both conceptual systems in conceptual space and actual systems in actual space, are the correct units of analysis, and there are shearing layers not only within conceptual space and within actual space but also between conceptual space and actual space? In such a model, what would the function of language be, and how would concepts and ideas be constructed?

I think that the mistake *words mean things* is connected to the way we prioritise logic and definition over abstraction and analogy in our models of rational thinking. Logic and definition give form but not substance to thinking. They will help you think clearly using a conceptual structure, but they won't create the contents of that structure. The content is the outcome of the processes of abstraction and analogy.

I have come to the view that the model of compositionalism, of parts and wholes, does not work and that, therefore, reductive and deterministic explanations in the style of scientific materialism and holistic and idealist explanations in the Platonic tradition are both mistaken and that an alternative model of the world can and should be constructed: a model of the world as a system of intersecting systems, multi-layered, indeterminate and open-ended; operating at different scales, changing at a varying paces, and evolving according to multiple ordering principles. Once we have stopped imposing compositional structures on our experience, the innately open-ended and fluid characteristics of the world can become apparent.

In order to understand the ramifications of this idea we first need to re-model two sets of ideas. The first set is organised around the idea of composition: change, identity, process, scale, pacing and order. The second set is organised around the idea of abstraction: type, analogy, map and model. Applied to domains as diverse as science and ethics, these models make space for a different way of thinking about nature, about intelligence and about practical reasoning, and therefore also about our place in the universe both as observers and participants.

CHAPTER TWO

# THE IDEA IS CRYSTALLINE, THE FACT FLUID

## Systems, populations, objects & stuff

We habitually think of composition in terms of parts and wholes, but this schema is too simple to capture the diversity in the construction and behaviour of composite entities. We need a better model in order to bring out the differences.

If we take two characteristics of composite entities: the degree of similarity of the components and the degree of cohesiveness in the structure; then we can build a model with four types of entity. Applying the test of similarity to the components of cohesive structures, we generate the distinction between *objects* and *stuff*. Objects are constructed out of components of different types, whereas a sample of some stuff is constructed through the aggregation of a single type of component. Applying the same test of similarity to less cohesive collections, we generate the distinction between *systems* and *populations*. The distinction here is the same: systems are composed of many types of component, whereas populations are composed of just one type.

Objects and systems are both composed of many types of component, but an object is a relatively cohesive structure whereas a system is a much looser entity. In the same way, a sample of some stuff and a population are both composed of components of a single type, but the sample is a relatively cohesive structure while a population may be very loosely organised, if it is organised at all. A population may exist only in the mind of an observer.

Objects are cohesive entities composed of components of different types. If you decompose an object into its constituent parts the result will be a set of heterogeneous components. An object is typically a modular structure. Most living organisms and most artefacts can be thought of as modular structures in this sense. My guess is that when we talk about *things*, it is this type of composition that we have in mind.

The word 'module' originally meant a small or allotted measure, but in modern usage it has come to have a meaning something like an interchangeable or reusable part. Typically, a modular structure is a whole constructed from a number of parts, where each performs a discrete function. Modular structures are therefore usually functional wholes, such that the functions that support the whole are distributed among the components, with each component performing a task for the benefit of the whole. If we think about a building, for example, we can point to the foundations, the walls, the roof, the doors and windows, the cables and conduits, the partitions and the furniture. The building has a function, and the form of the building and the materials used in its construction are related to the function. Each of the components has a function which contributes to the whole: defining the volume; bearing the loads; weatherproofing; defining and enabling the circulation of people, materials and services.

Although both mechanical and organic structures are usually thought of as modular, there is a significant difference in how they are constructed. Mechanical structures are typically assembled: the parts are constructed separately and then the whole is put together from the component parts. The components of a mechanical structure can be highly diverse in form, material and function. Each component of a mechanical structure can be replaced with an upgraded version independently of the whole of which it is a part, which is why modularity is an indispensable idea in modern industrial production.

Organic structures tend to grow such that additional components are formed through processes of extension, division and differentiation rather than through processes of assembly. The parts don't exist prior to the whole. Rather, the whole extends, divides and diversifies. The components of an organic structure often differ in function, but looked at closely there are repetitions of form and material. For this reason, a mechanical structure is more easily modelled reductively than an organic structure, which is more plausibly understood holistically.

However, the distinction can be overloaded with a significance it doesn't have. Traditional agrarian technologies are also mechanical; a modern wind turbine is not really a different kind of construction from a traditional windmill; and many advances in medicine, physiology and genetic engineering are based on applying a mechanical understanding to living organisms.

If objects are typically modular structures, samples of stuff are typically cellular structures. Like a modular structure, a cellular structure is a cohesive entity, but one that is built up through the repetition of components that have the same form.

The term 'cell' originally came from the idea of a small room. It was first applied to the partitions in monastic dormitories and later to the small rooms in prisons, and then by association to compartments in general and from there to the basic unit of living organisms. Stuff is constitutive; the tissue or fabric that gives everything its bulk and extension is constructed through the repetition of components that have the same form.

Because every object's heft, its physical mass and extension, comes from the stuff from which it is made, every modular structure is also a cellular structure, the two types of organisation folded together in alternating layers. For example, a living organism, which is modular, is composed of tissues, which are stuff, which are in turn composed of cells, which are modular.

A cellular structure is a sample of some *stuff* rather than an instance of some *thing*. Because stuff is built up through repetition, when you decompose a cellular aggregate into its constitutive components, they are all of the same kind: heaps of grains; lumps of earth; streams and pools of water; clouds of gas; cell tissues; the crystalline lattices that are the solid state of matter; fabrics of woven cloth; ropes of plaited fibres; honeycombs; the bricks in a wall.

Modular and cellular structures are relatively cohesive structures, in contrast to systems and populations, which are more integrated. Systems, like modular structures, tend to contain a large number of different types of components. But whereas in a modular structure there is a distribution of function, in a system there is a distribution of control or decision-making. In a modular structure each component has a role within the structure and collaborates with other components to achieve a shared function; in a system, each component has its own organising principle and the components must therefore adjust, accommodate and adapt to each other.

System boundaries are rarely clearly defined. To the gardener the boundaries of the garden are important, but they probably don't register to the bees that pollinate the flowers. An ecosystem can be thought of as a population of living organisms interacting with each other and with the natural environment. Similarly, urban environments are complex networks of interactions between the inhabitants, the built environment and the natural environment. If we were drawing a diagram, the system boundaries would almost always be dotted lines.

Mechanical constructions like aircraft, no matter how complicated, tend to remain mechanical constructions, but organic structures can be transformed into systems through extension, division and differentiation. This is also what happens to buildings, which are conceived as modular wholes in the architect's drawings but become systems as differences in the pace of change fracture the integrity of the original structure. A building, viewed in terms of principle of composition, occupies a place somewhere between mechanical assembly and organic differentiation.

A population, like a cellular structure, is composed of components that are all the same type. The difference is that a population is much less integrated than a sample of stuff, and may not be integrated at all. A population of trees will compose a forest, but the global population of trees doesn't compose a global forest. The concept of a population is closely connected to the concept of a type. A population is a collection of entities of the same type, and it is for this reason that populations may exist only in the mind of an observer: the global population of trees and the global population of buildings do not form any kind of structure or system.

A cellular structure deconstructed becomes a population. A collection of bricks may be stacked on a pallet in rows, left as a heap in the middle of the brickyard, or arranged in linear fashion to form a wall. Stacks, heaps and walls are all cellular structures, and all are possible configurations of the population of bricks, but they are all inherently transitory. The individual bricks continue to exist however they are configured, and the population of bricks exists independently of any possible organisation.

Thus far, this analysis has been static. Entities exist in the synchronic perspective, to borrow a term from structuralism; that is, they describe the state of the system at a moment in time. To achieve the diachronic perspective, and see the evolution of the structure through time and the history of the transitions between states, we need to think in terms of events. The synchronic and the diachronic perspectives must go together – for *who can know the dancer from the dance?* – but it is only from the diachronic perspective that the ramifications of composition really become apparent. In the synchronic perspective, events happen to entities. In the diachronic perspective entities form, are transformed, and then dissipate in the course of events. In the diachronic perspective, entities are seen to be events.

We often miss the diachronic because we observe and measure the pace of change at the human scale. Fast-changing and slow-changing are speeds relative to our experience. Many systems move too slowly for us to see the transformations, at least without the aid of instruments such as time-lapse photography. But once you start thinking about composite entities from the diachronic perspective, as transient configurations of components, the fluidity of the world starts to become apparent. It becomes clear that because everything is composite, everything is transient.

This fluidity poses the problem of identity. The identity of composite entities is not easily grasped; it is variable, transitory and indeterminate, maybe even an illusion. For this reason, the familiar observable world of composite entities has always been problematic. In modern physics composite structures have largely been left behind as the units of analysis, to be replaced by fields and forces. However, even before modern science there has been a strong tendency in Western thinking to posit an unchanging structure beyond, behind or within the familiar world of experience.

In much Eastern thinking everything composite is an illusion, or, perhaps more accurately, the illusory nature of the world is a consequence of its composite structure. In Buddhism even the self is an illusion. Attachment to composite things is attachment to what is transitory, and therefore necessarily the way to dissatisfaction. The path to liberation is therefore the path to a state of detachment from the composite world, thereby constraining this attachment.

But perhaps, as with architects thinking about buildings, our unit of analysis has always been wrong. Perhaps we have imposed the attributes of the conceptual world on the actual world and then found this to be a problem. We think of thought as malleable and fluid and the physical world as fixed and unmoving, when in fact it's the opposite. Brand says of building that *'the idea is crystalline, the fact fluid'*. This implies that there is a shearing layer between conceptual space, which is relatively structured and static, and actual space, which is relatively unstructured and dynamic, and the error has always been to impose the characteristics of the one upon the other.

## The indeterminacy of identity

There are perhaps two basic challenges to establishing the identity of anything, which might be called 'the problem of composition' and 'the problem of gradualness'.

One of the oldest thought experiments about the identity of things is called the ship of Theseus. It's a thought experiment that was first recorded by Plutarch, writing in the 1st century. The idea is this. Imagine a wooden sailing vessel. Pieces are replaced as they break or wear out, and it's possible to imagine that, over time, every component is replaced so that the ship contains none of its original parts. When this happens, is it still the same ship, or is it a different one? If it's a different one, at which point did the change occur? In the 17th century Thomas Hobbes added a further refinement to the thought experiment. Suppose that the pieces that have been replaced are kept in store and repaired, and sometime later a whole new ship is re-assembled from these original parts. There could now be two ships, both of which would appear to have a reasonable claim to being the original.

Various solutions have been proposed to the puzzle, but my interpretation is that it demonstrates that we have at least two models of identity. The first model is in terms of composition. Something that is made from the same components is the same thing even when there is no continuity in its existence. Things can retain their identity through the disassembly and re-assembly of the components. This might be called the 'compositional model' of identity.

The second model of identity is in terms of process. When we replace a component, we don't typically think that we have something new. As long as we replace only a few components at a time, we will tend to the view that we still have the same thing, even if, as in the case of the ship in the thought experiment, over time every piece is replaced. This might be called the 'process model' of identity. Something can retain its identity even if every component is replaced, so long as the process happens step by step and some continuity persists throughout.

The thought experiment can be replayed with some more modern technology. Suppose you take a car in for repair and the workshop strips it down, lays the pieces out on the workbench, and then puts it back together again, perhaps replacing a few worn-out parts. Would you regard it as the same machine? Probably yes. But suppose that instead of being laid out on the workbench the components are placed in the parts bins and then some time later another car is assembled from similar components picked from the same bins. Is it now the same machine? Perhaps not. We have different intuitions about these kinds of questions, and you can play with the experiment to discover how your intuitions fall. It seems likely, however, that at some point there is going to be sufficient disruption to the continuity of identity to justify saying that we no longer have the same object.

Process identity is more common than compositional identity. The built environment has primarily process identity, buildings are extended and adapted, and so, as a consequence of modularisation, are the outputs of modern industrial production.

The quicker processes of repair, alteration and replacement happen within the slower processes of extension and development, disintegration and dispersal. Living organisms, including human beings, have primarily process identity. Like buildings, living beings are composed of multiple layers of longevity, and few of the components that make up an organism will last a lifetime. The quick processes of metabolism and cell regeneration take place within the slower processes of growth and development. These modifications are usually gradual, although some living organisms, such as butterflies, do pass through a metamorphosis, a sudden and disruptive change of form. The population of living organisms also undergoes continuous adaptation as the distribution of characteristics and traits is modified in the processes of evolutionary change.

And it is not just that the form is retained while the components change, because form, like composition, is dynamic. Entities can retain their identity through the complete turnover of components and substantial modification of form, as long as the changes are gradual.

In that sense the problem of composition is therefore one form of the problem of gradualness. The problem of gradualness also has a long history, and in general form it is called the *sorites* problem, from the Greek term for a heap. The idea is this. Imagine a heap of grains of sand. If just one grain of sand is removed it will still be the same heap and this will continue to be the case if you remove more grains of sand one by one. But remove enough grains of sand and the heap will be gone. The problem is that it doesn't seem possible to identify the disappearance of the heap with the removal of any one particular grain of sand.

The degree of disruption required to rupture either or both compositional and process identity demonstrates a graduated dimension. The ship of Theseus is the problem of gradualness applied to the identity of modular structures and systems, because the question is just how many parts can be replaced before one thing becomes something else. The sorites problem is the problem of gradualness applied to cellular structures and populations. As with the puzzle of the ship of Theseus, the thought experiment provokes recognition rather than demanding a solution. What is being recognised is the indeterminateness of identity, an indeterminateness that is a consequence of composition.

In fact, the problem of gradualness applies not only to the composition of an entity, but also to its state and boundaries. The transitions from young to old, from poor to rich, from small to large are graduated state changes, and the expansion and contraction of a system is a graduated shifting of its boundaries.

These thought experiments about identity through change can also be applied to the possibility of alternative paths that the course of events might take. These might be counterfactual speculations about past events or the anticipation and evaluation of possible future events. If we think about how events might have taken a different course, how different do the events have to be before we stop thinking of them as an alternative history of one thing and start to think of them as the history of something else?

This is important for our own idea of ourselves. How different would our life have to be for us to consider ourselves a different person? There seem to be two mistakes possible here. The first is to be too rigid, and to suppose that had our lives been in any way different we would be a different person. The second type of error is to be too flexible and to suppose that, since every path starts from the same place, we will be the same person no matter how different our lives turn out to be. The first polarity is to think that the course of events in a lifetime contributes everything, the second that the course of events in a lifetime contributes nothing.

If neither of these ideas is persuasive it becomes more plausible to think of the identity of a person not just as one history or as all the histories that started from the same point of origin, but more as a kind of envelope of possible histories, and imagine that who we are is not just the path we did take but also some of the paths we did not take. Some of these alternative paths were very close to the actual path; they were paths we might quite easily have taken, and taking them would not have provoked a rupture. Others are more distant and disruptive and were therefore much less likely to happen. Such an envelope of possibility would itself be indeterminate, having no clear boundary, but flattening out into the infinitely remote and the infinitely improbable.

## Populations and types

The indeterminateness of identity isn't a consequence of an epistemological limitation, a limitation of knowability, in the way that, for example, quantum indeterminacy is thought to be. The indeterminateness of identity persists although the boundaries and state of an event or entity are known. The source of the difficulty lies in the limitations of language and therefore, because ideas are built out of language, this is also a limitation to what is thinkable. This limitation is a function of the difference between events and entities in conceptual space and events and entities in actual space. The crux of the problem is a generalisation of the issue that Stewart Brand identified when thinking about buildings: *the idea is crystalline, the fact fluid.*

Indeterminateness of identity doesn't normally trouble us because we usually don't attempt to capture in ideas and words the totality of things. Instead we think and speak in abstractions. Abstraction is the process of discarding information from concepts in order to create types, and abstraction into types is the simple solution to the problem of indeterminateness thrown up by composition and gradualness. Types map to populations, so that in identifying the type of something we also identify the population to which it belongs.

Some concepts are extremely abstract. The concepts *entity* and *event* for instance are about as abstract as you can get, because almost every distinguishing attribute has been discarded, leaving only the idea that something is distinguishable. But I think it is a mistake to think that there are any concepts that are not abstract – that is, that there are concrete concepts. The way this distinction is usually drawn is to say, for example, that the idea *house* is abstract but the idea *the White House* is concrete. But a moment's thought will show that while the concept *house* applies to a population of objects and must therefore be an abstraction, the concept *the White House* must also be an abstraction, because it refers to the same building through time and the building is constantly changing, some components more rapidly than others. We can also imagine an alternative history for the building in an alternative history of the world and still have no problem applying the idea *the White House* in this counterfactual story.

It is possible to have entities and events where the specification is the totality of the entity. This is the case with cultural artefacts that don't have a physical existence or any physical correlates. A financial instrument, for example, has no physical existence; it is entirely described by the terms of the trade. There is nothing else, nothing from which the specification has been abstracted. In these cases, the specification does describe the totality of the object. Nevertheless, the description doesn't constitute the trade. This can be demonstrated by thinking about what would happen if you duplicated the description; you would have two descriptions, but still just one trade.

The problem with the way the distinction between abstract and concrete is drawn is that it conflates two different questions: the size of the population that the term applies to, and the depth of detail in the specification. There is a link between the two, in that, for a given specification, the more detail that is added, the smaller the population of entities or events that it will apply to. But they are not correlated, because the level of detail required to map to a single thing is contingent on circumstances.

Abstraction is the solution not just to the problem of how we ignore the differences and focus on the similarities when we are thinking about populations, but equally how we can ignore the differences and focus on the similarities when we are thinking about a single entity changing through time or across alternative histories. It is as a consequence of abstraction that we can talk about populations, identity through time and identity across counterfactual and imagined histories. In each case, abstraction allows us to recognise sameness within difference. Without abstraction into types it wouldn't be possible to have populations of things except where each member of the population was an exact copy or replica of every other member of the population. Similarly, because things change it would not be possible without abstraction to recognise the persistence of entities through time or speculate on alternative paths that the course of events might have taken.

Abstraction is really a process. It is the process of removing information from a description or specification in order to create a type. The more abstract the specification, the less information it contains, so *building* is a more abstract type that *house*, and *living organism* is a more abstract type than *human being*.

The relationship between population and type is the intersection between composition and classification. The quantity of information contained in a specification and the size of the population to which the specification applies are inversely related. The more abstract the type the larger the population and, conversely, the less abstract the type the smaller the population. For example, the specification of the type *event* will provide the least possible amount of information and apply to the widest possible population. The population of events includes everything distinguishable by some criteria. However, at the other end of the scale there is no limit to the amount of information that can be included in the specification of a type. The limit isn't a type that applies to only one event, but specifications that are so laden with detail that they don't actually apply to anything.

Types are organised into hierarchies. These hierarchies are perhaps easier to see looked at from the alternative perspective of populations. The relationship between population and sub-population is one of containment or inclusion. For example, the global population of buildings contains the global population of houses. It also contains, among many others, the global population of factories and the global population of warehouses. Types and sub-types work through the relationship of containment in the same way but inversely. The specifications of the types for *house*, *factory* and *warehouse* all contain the specification for the type *building*. What is contained is the set of attributes and the set of values that compose the specification together with the rules that govern how these are constructed. Attributes and values are the primary components of a type. The type *house* contains all the shared attributes and values that compose the specification for buildings, plus all the specific attributes and values that apply only to houses. Similarly, the type *factory* contains the specification for buildings plus the additional information specific to factories; and the type *warehouse* contains the specification for buildings plus the additional information specific to warehouses.

This relationship of containment, when it is modelled in computer software, is called inheritance, and it is the inheritance of attributes and values that binds together the type-hierarchy. A specification can inherit from more than one hierarchy. For example, the specification for *house* inherits from the specification for *building* but also from the specification for *dwelling*. As a building it is part of the same population as factories and warehouses; as a dwelling it is part of the same population as apartments, tents and houseboats.

The same pattern applies to natural objects. If *event* is the most abstract type and can be applied to any distinguishable thing, then the distinction between *artefact* and *natural* might be at the next level of abstraction down. Everything that is part of nature inherits from the type *natural object*. *Living organism* inherits from *natural object* and *animal* and *plant* inherit from *living organism*. Inheriting from the type *living organism* implies that the specification of an animal or plant includes, among others things, that it is composed of cells, is a component of the biosphere, has a position on the tree of life and is the outcome of an evolutionary process. It is important to recognise that these attributes and values belong to the part of the specification that is common across living organisms, not to the part that is specific to animals or specific to plants.

A population is a collection of things of the same type. The type is its specification. It answers the question: what class of entities or events does this population of entities and events belong to? Types are much looser than definitions. A definition is a set of necessary and sufficient conditions for membership of a population. Types, on the other hand, function to capture what Wittgenstein called 'family resemblance'.

In their paper on *Kuhn's mature philosophy of science and cognitive psychology*, Hanne Andersen, Peter Barker and Xiang Chen argue that it is in psychology rather than philosophy that a naturalistic theory of concept formation has been developed:

> *The rejection by Wittgenstein, and later by Kuhn, of the traditional view that concepts can be defined by necessary and sufficient conditions, came into psychology in the mid-1970s by the research carried out by Eleanor Rosch and her collaborators. It is difficult to convey to philosophers the completeness of the change in psychologists' theories of concepts brought about by this work. Although there were studies prior to Rosch's that indicated similar effects...it is generally acknowledged that the work of Rosch and her collaborators was primarily responsible for dis-establishing the account of concepts based on necessary and sufficient conditions, and replacing it with a consensus view that is*

> *basically Wittgenstein's, even if its detailed structure is still a matter for debate.*

Eleanor Rosch developed the psychological model of concept formation called 'prototype theory'. Prototype theory proposes that for every concept there is central image that functions as the model, the prototype. Potential members of a population are then evaluated against their similarity to this prototype.

The difference between prototypes, which anchor family resemblances, and definitions, which specify necessary and sufficient conditions, can be illustrated with the concept *house*. A house is both a building and a dwelling: it has the form of a building and functions as a dwelling. But several other dimensions are significant: scale, unity and permanence. Houses are larger than shacks and smaller than mansions. A house is not a subdivided building in the way that an apartment block is. And a house is designed to be permanently occupied, unlike say a cabin or lodge.

Such a specification along at least five incommensurable axes will quickly throw up ambiguous and borderline cases. Sometimes it may be important to remove ambiguity – in order, for example, to establish building regulations or tax codes. This can be done by stipulating a definition, as in a legal document the specific meaning of a given term or phrase in the context of the document is stipulated. But in most everyday usage there is no need to do this.

## Maps and analogues

Abstraction, which is a process of ignoring, is a powerful technique. But how can an abstract conceptual model – say, a model labelled *building* or *garden*, built out of words or numbers – be applied to events and entities to bring into view actual buildings and gardens? Something is required to bridge the gap. This is the difficulty of the meaning of words. How do words apply to anything? How can an arbitrary string of signs or sounds, patterns of disturbance in a medium, have a meaning?

The answer is through mapping and analogy. Conceptually, the simplest kind of mapping is copying. The attributes of one copy will map one-to-one to the attributes of another thing that is a copy of it. But copying is very limited in scope and allows mapping only across broadly similar forms. Something additional is required in order to map across differences and make possible the application of abstract conceptual entities to actual events and entities. I think that what makes this possible is the capacity for analogy.

An analogue is a kind of copy, but one where the copy has been transformed through changes in form, proportions, scale, material composition and presentation. The plan of the London Underground is a good example of this process. The plan is on a wholly different scale from the transport system and ignores most of its features, but the relationship between lines, stations and interchanges is retained through the transformation into symbols on a piece of a paper.

The distinction between copy and a map can be illustrated by considering the difference between a map and a reference sample. We use reference samples for purposes such as colour matching and weighing and measuring. We can use samples as a means of referencing simple objects as long as the reference sample is a near copy. A map, on the other hand, can be quite unlike the original in form, but because the structural relationships are retained it remains an analogue and can therefore function as a map.

The identification of one object as the map and the other as the territory is a convention. There is a usually a mismatch in the level of information in the entities at each end of the mapping. When we make a model, we usually reduce the level of information. When we build something from a blueprint or technical drawing, we usually increase the amount of information. We tend to regard the more abstract version, the one where the scale and the density of information has been reduced, as the map, but there are circumstances in which it is the other way around. However, normally the more abstract entity is the map because unnecessary information is noise, and noise disguises signal. A noisy map isn't usually very useful.

At the limit one end of the mapping may be a very schematic analogue of the other end. The plan of the London Underground functions well as a map just because it is schematic. One thing it says is: don't be afraid of schematics – in Alfred Korzybski's dictum, the map is not the territory.

There is a gradient from copy to analogue. Copies are more or less similar in form and analogues are potentially quite different in form. In defining analogy in this way, I have in mind the example of topology in mathematics where properties are preserved through distortion. In the case of an analogue the properties which map are preserved through transformations in form, scale, rendering and composition among others.

To function as an analogue a map must have the same number of possible states as the terrain, the target domain, at the relevant level of abstraction. If a system, such as a switch, has two possible states, *off* and *on*, there must be two possible states of the map, perhaps *zero* and *one*. A complex system, such as natural language or visual imagery, may have an uncountable number of possible states, and any map must have the same capacity.

A map that included every piece of information in the original would be a copy and of little value as a map. Lewis Carroll played with this idea, and Jorge Luis Borges wrote a number of stories on the theme of the map and the territory, including one called *On Exactitude in Science,* about a land in which the cartographers guild made a map of the empire that was the same size as the empire, which was then found to be completely useless.

The application of concepts to actual events and entities is a mapping. The type *house* applies to a particular building because each attribute in the type maps one-to-one to a feature of the entity. If I were to try to map the type *boat* to the same location, I would have some success because boats share some features with houses, but I will not find a keel, a prow or running gear, and I will quickly realise that the conceptual structure *boat* doesn't apply to the fragment of the universe in front of me at this level of abstraction. It doesn't coincide point for point. But at a higher level of abstraction in the type-hierarchy, say at the level of *construction* or *artefact*, the same type will map both to houses and to boats. At the highest levels of abstraction, the mapping may not be according to form, function or material composition at all, but may be instead a question of origin, purpose or life-cycle.

The link between types and populations is not the only relationship built out of mappings and analogies. What is the relationship between the members of a population? I think the answer is also that the members of a population are analogues. This is easier to see when the objects, such as leaves and banknotes, are very similar and there is, with very little abstraction, a one-to-one mapping between every feature. But analogy, as in the case of buildings, can survive deformation and distortion and transformations in the level of abstraction, scale and rendering.

A third example of the power of analogy is the modern digital computer. Modern computing is made possible by the recognition of the analogy that can be found between logical and algebraic operations on binary inputs and the way transistors function to switch voltages. A transistor in an electronic circuit can function either as a switch or an amplifier. When it is working as a switch, a low voltage input is switched to a high voltage output and a high voltage input to a low voltage output. This is an analogue, that is, it maps one to one, with the logical operation of negation on binary inputs, where the negation of zero is one and the negation of one is zero.

Abstraction and analogy are in my view the primary intellectual processes, and definition and logical inference are secondary in sequence and importance. Abstraction is necessary to find the sameness in difference: without the possibility of abstraction, only totalities could be comprehended and thinking would be more or less impossible. Similarly, analogy is necessary to map across differences: without the possibility of analogy, mapping could not survive the changes in scale and the transformations and distortions required to make a useful map.

Only after concepts have been created and applied in the processes of abstraction and analogy can we follow processes of logical inference. And in order to make logical inferences, types need to be constrained as definitions. For a logical inference to be valid, the variables $p$ and $q$ must refer to the same specification throughout the inference. The same necessity applies to algebra, so that $a$ and $b$ must remain the same quantity throughout the algorithm.

# Labelling the maps

Language exists only as a performance. If we draw an analogy with the way computer software functions, language is a type of communication program, words are the content of the database, and syntax is a set of rules and principles used to structure the communication. Every instance of someone speaking, writing, listening or reading is a run-time event; a specific execution of the language program in the course of which words in the database are selected and applied in a particular situation. It is almost always necessary to improvise and adapt the words to the circumstances. The flexibility of language comes from the fact that it is in this sense a performance. In the performance a pattern is imposed on the flow of words in the same way that shapes are formed in the play of water from a fountain.

In the *Philosophical Investigations*, Wittgenstein called these performances language-games and the activities of which they are a component forms-of-life. Language is an inexhaustible fountain because there is no stock of words to be used and used up:

> *But how many kinds of sentence are there? Say assertion, question, command? — There are countless kinds: countless different kinds of use of what we call 'symbols', 'words', 'sentences'. And this multiplicity is not something fixed once for all; but new types of language, new language-games, as we may say, come into existence, and other becomes obsolete and get forgotten... Here the term 'language-game'*

> is meant to bring into prominence the fact that the speaking of language is part of an activity, or a form of life.

Language-games and forms-of-life are performances. What isn't in Wittgenstein's account, but can be added, is that we can say that abstraction and mapping are language-games in the form-of-life called conceptual thinking.

This idea that words acquire their meaning in use doesn't imply any arbitrariness, any sense that words can mean whatever we want them to mean. And we don't need to suppose that there is a kind of endless deferral of meaning in the way that Jacques Derrida suggested. Although every new use, and every reuse, and every forgetting (if we are able to determine when lack of use turns into forgetting) makes a difference to the population of performances and therefore a modification to the meaning, these modifications will quickly become marginal adjustments to the map and will rarely be material when we consider the inherent indeterminateness implied in applying the map to the terrain.

If language is always a performance and acquires its flexibility in use, where does the stability come from? I think the answer is from the stability of our conceptual models. Conceptual space is composed of abstract models. Because they are abstractions, conceptual models are much more stable than actual entities and events: *the idea is crystalline, the fact fluid*.

It is because they are abstractions that it is possible to apply the same conceptual model to multiple entities and events. We use words as labels for the components of these models. Words cannot be used easily as labels in actual space because the entities and events are too fluid and ambiguous. However, words can be applied through the application of stable conceptual models acting as intermediaries. Words can be used as labels in conceptual space because the abstract models that populate conceptual space have been defined, determined and stipulated in order that they become relatively stable, relatively unambiguous structures.

But even so, conceptual modelling is itself also a performance. Conceptual models only appear to be static because they usually change slowly, and at a different pace from the actual world. There is a shearing layer between our conceptual architecture and the world we inhabit. But our conceptual models do evolve, and we have been engaged in a history-long collaboration making, modifying, safeguarding and transmitting the conceptual structures that we apply every time that we speak or write.

Because words are abstractions, it is almost impossible to communicate the particularity of something in descriptive speech and writing, the kind that we use for critical and forensic thinking and for science and philosophy. Critical and forensic thinking is concerned with the structures of conceptual space and the way they can be applied to particular events. However, words can be made to go beyond these limitations, in the way that music and the visual arts do, in evocative speech and writing, in fiction, drama and poetry and, somewhat differently, in writing history. In these disciplines, words are being used to evoke the particularity of an event or entity and to make it significant through this particularity rather than through its type.

One consequence of the abstraction of language is that we can fail to see what is in front of us because there is always a conceptual structure mediating our relationship to the actual world. The world tends to look familiar because we apply familiar structures in order to interpret it. There is therefore a value in sometimes trying to de-familiarise the world by applying unexpected models. We can't conceptualise an unmediated fact but we can escape the limitations of the familiar by overlaying counter-intuitive conceptual structures.

Words are the most important vehicles for the construction and communication of conceptual models. An utterance is composed of strings of words. A small number of words (*and, or, but* and so on) are used to structure discourse, but most of the terms in a lexicon are used to build conceptual models and apply them to actual entities and events. These words fall into five categories according to the function they serve: classification, pointing, selection, quantification and naming.

Most of the terms in any language are classifications. Words apply to types and therefore to populations: they classify what type of entity or event something is and therefore which population it belongs to. However, by themselves classifications have no application. They articulate the configuration of a conceptual model but they don't say anything about the configuration of the actual world. When we want to apply a conceptual model to actual entities and events, we have to use another set of terms to point to, to make a selection from, or to specify the quantity of, a population.

Pointers are terms used to identify an actual population to which we are referring, and the words that we use to do this are a kind of addressing mechanism, a verbal gesture: *this* thing, *here* and *now* rather than *that* thing, *there* and *then*. For example, we might say *'this house was built in the modernist style'*. Pronouns work in a similar way. The word *I* points to the speaker so that its meaning in a sentence depends on who is speaking, just as *now* and *then* depend on the moment in time and *here* and *there* on the location in space. These terms are called indexicals because they point to or index a specific population of events or entities rather than a class of events and entities. Selections and quantifications can be added to pointers to more narrowly focus the target. For example, the words *a, none, some, any, most* and *all* specify a selection or a quantity, so that we can then say, for example, *'some of these houses were constructed from pre-fabricated components'* or *'you can choose any book you like from the library'*.

These formulations can be cumbersome, and rather than continually repeating a description it can be simpler to give the target event or entity a name. Names have been philosophically problematic and I think the reason is that the use of names carries with it a number of unstated assumptions. There is a close connection between names and identities. An essentialist approach to identity will lead to an essentialist approach to names. If I am right that the function of abstraction is to track sameness not only within populations but also across changes in time and through counterfactual and imagined sequences of events, it follows that names are also abstractions. If a name were applied to a totality of an entity, it would cease to apply as soon as any attribute or value changed. Types track the sameness in difference across populations, and names track the sameness in difference of singular entities through their life-cycle.

One way in which we can think about names is as a sort of classification, where what is being classified is not a population of entities but a population of events. By giving something a name, we are assuming that a collection of occurrences are the multiple appearances of a single entity and not the singular appearances of multiple entities. Naming is a convention based on an assumption about what we are experiencing.

A nice example comes from William Goldman's novel *The Princess Bride* and the character of the Dread Pirate Roberts. This looks like a name and for a time we assume that the many appearances of the Dread Pirate Roberts are the many appearances of a single person, because that is what it means to bear a name. It is only later that we become aware that more than one person has been the Dread Pirate Roberts, and that it is actually a role rather than a person, and therefore that the words are a title and not a name.

Stories that turn on alter egos and identical twins impersonating each other similarly play with this convention. With the alter egos, we have fewer persons than we have names; with the identical twins we have more persons that we have names. However, we as readers often only know this because we have privileged information. This is how we know, although the other characters don't, that the multiple appearances of Superman and the multiple appearances of Clark Kent are in fact all appearances of just one entity.

Cultural artefacts such as novels, films and plays require a different model for names. What is the correct unit of analysis for a cultural artefact such as *King Lear*? Although this looks like the name of some 'thing', the superficial grammar is misleading. *King Lear* isn't an object in the sense that a painting or a piece of sculpture is an object. However, it isn't a type either in the way that, for example, tragedy is a type of theatre. We could classify all the copies of the text and all the productions as instances of the type *King Lear*, but this would miss a significant feature. The population of plays that we call tragedies have a number of similar characteristics but there is no necessary continuity between them. In contrast, the population of texts and theatrical representations that are the reference for the name *King Lear* have an historical continuity.

A better approach is to think in terms of repetitions. In this case the name applies to a population of events. From this perspective, *King Lear* isn't so much a type but rather can be thought of as a collective name for a set of repetitions or executions of a program. The program may be a performance of the play, where the text functions as storage and evidence, prompts and cues for the actors, the director and the crew; however, the population of performances also contains every occasion on which someone has read through the text of the play to themselves. Because it is a population, indeterminateness applies. How much can a work be adapted, modified, truncated, mashed-up and re-interpreted before it ceases to be part of the same population and therefore should no longer bear the same name?

A useful analogy here is with a piece of software. The execution of a computer program is the performance of a set of instructions. Each execution of the code is an independent performance driven by the sequence of instructions acting on the inputs that are to hand.

The boundary between using names and using descriptions isn't fixed, and some of the time we get to choose. There are too many things for everything to have a name; we typically give the forest a name, but not the individual trees. Information technology may drive the naming of many more things. The serial number on a bank note is a name, as is the vehicle identification number etched on a car's window. A language without names would be impossibly cumbersome, a language just of names impossibly limited. Names don't change frequently because their usefulness would be compromised if they did, but they do shift about, fall into disuse, and their references get modified. The use of names is driven primarily by convenience.

Descriptions carry information about the type, attributes and values of things. Therefore, if you have the description, you should be able to identify the reference. Names often start out as descriptions but then get left behind by change. Because they don't carry information, names can remain the same while the entity named can change. However, for the same reason, names have to be applied in the equivalent of a naming ceremony, and the use of the name transmitted in a sort of chain of custody from speaker to speaker, otherwise it will not be possible to understand what is being referred to.

How should we model this? Unlike a type, a name implies some level of historical continuity. Names are a kind of empty specification. A person's name contains no necessary descriptive information to add to the information contained within the type-hierarchy: human being, living organism, natural object and so on. The specification in the type-hierarchy for 'person' is extensive and the name itself does not add any new information, it is just a convenient label for a particular instance. Names as such don't carry any descriptive information, but they are still located in an implicit type-hierarchy. The way people bear names differs from the way that mountains, rivers and lakes, or constructions such as boats, structures such as bridges and cultural artefacts such as novels and plays do. The way the name is borne is inherited from the type of entity that it is and how we expect it to change through time.

Quantification is the particular kind of abstract modelling built out of counts and measures. In a quantified model all the information about the system is discarded except the information that can be rendered in numerical form. Populations are counted and stuff is measured. Measurement is really a form of counting, but one where an artificial unit, such as a metre, is overlain on a sample of some stuff, and then these artificial units are counted. Counting and measuring is thought to have pre-dated numbering. Originally counts and measures could have been recorded by making a tally mark for each item in the population, and from there the number of marks could be compared with that from another count or measure, allowing a quantitative comparison.

In that way tallying is to numbers as gesturing and the use of samples is to words. Tallying is analogous to the use of reference samples with regard to colours. We have trouble distinguishing colours by eye without a reference sample, and also struggle for accuracy and precision with quantities without a reference measure. We are good at comparison but bad at absolute magnitudes.

Counts and ratios are quantities without any dimension or unit. Measurements on the other hand have an associated dimension and unit, and homogenising the dimensions and units is a requirement for manipulating the quantities. In scientific models the basic dimensions are length, time, mass, charge and temperature. In financial models the basic dimensions are time and money.

There are two levels of abstraction possible with quantitative models. At the first level of abstraction all the attributes of an entity or event are disregarded except those that are countable and measurable. In the scientific revolution of the 17th century these came to be thought of as the primary attributes of objects. At this level we are still concerned with the properties of objects, but slippage from the first level to the second level of abstraction is inevitable. For example, Galileo began teaching mathematics at Pisa in 1589, and his notes show that at that time he was teaching that the speed of a falling object is proportional to its density rather than its weight, as was thought in the Aristotelian science of the time. He is supposed to have demonstrated this by dropping objects of the same weight but different densities from the nearby tower.

However, already the objects are redundant; we don't need to know what they were to follow the story. The experiment really only requires weights and volumes and the measurement of times and distances. At this second level, we cease to be concerned with measuring the attributes of the objects as such, and instead focus only on the properties of the system: its extent and duration and the location and configuration of masses within it.

The same thing applies with financial models. One way to approach this is to think about the difference between the stock book and the ledger. The quantities in the stock book apply to the inventory, so that there is always something actual that the numbers refer to; there should always be a one-to-one mapping between a quantity in the stock book and an item of inventory in the warehouse. The quantities in the ledger, on the other hand, don't necessarily refer to anything tangible. The books and records of a company are designed to give a description of its financial position, not a description of its physical footprint.

If we apply this analogy to nature, we can ask the same question: is natural science the accounting view or the stock book view of the universe? The stock book view of science is the one that underwrites what might be called scientific realism. This view regards particle physics as continuous with the observable world, only more fine-grained and at a micro-scale. The alternative perspective is that particle physics is a model in mathematical form of a physical system more akin to a financier's view of a company or an economist's model of the national economy. It is a kind of balance sheet accounting of the universe, a re-conceptualisation in mathematical terms, but a balance sheet where the dimensions are extents and durations, masses and charges, fields and forces.

At the first level of abstraction we will be concerned with the quantities in the stock book perspective, and at the second level of abstraction we will be concerned with quantities from the accounting perspective. In the stock book perspective, we are interested in the properties of the objects in the system, whereas in the accounting perspective we are concerned with the distribution of quantities in the system. In this way, quantitative modelling leads to the disappearance from view of the objects of familiar experience.

## A theory is just a model

The scientific revolution begins with the decision to simplify the description of objects to focus only on primary attributes, the attributes that can be counted and measured. This was the move to the first level of quantified abstraction. Modern scientific thinking, particularly in physics, has now developed to a level of abstraction that has no place for objects. It has stepped over the boundary to the second level of abstraction.

Underlying this way of thinking is an idea about theoretical modelling. This is how Peter Godfrey-Smith describes theoretical modelling in his book *Theory and Reality*:

> *We might think of a model as a structure that is intended to represent another structure by virtue of an abstract similarity relationship between them… A good model is one that has some kind of similarity relationship, probably of an abstract kind, with the system that the model is "targeted" at…*

However, Godfrey-Smith also says:

> *Models have a different kind of representational relationship with the world from that found in language.*

I don't think this can be right. My view, and one of the load-bearing arguments of this essay, is that language's representational relationship with the world is similar to that of every other kind of model. Language, at least at the level of sophistication at which we use it, makes most sense thought of as the labelling system for a conceptual model composed of interrelated types that has a kind of similarity relationship with the actual world that is its target, its domain of application.

A type is a model, a conceptual model built out of language. Words are the labels for types, and for the attributes and values that are the components of the conceptual model. Like all models, a type has a different form from the original to which it is applied. Scale models are built from different materials and, obviously, on different scales. Maps, diagrams and graphs are symbolic representations in visual form. The balance sheet and the income and expense account model a business in terms of monetary values. In fact, mapping and modelling mean much the same: maps map and models model, but these are basically the same relationship, one of abstraction, analogy and application.

My justification for saying that language models concepts is practical rather than theoretical. The practice I have in mind is the development of descriptive schemas that software developers create to specify and structure the information in the databases used by computer systems and the messages passed between them. Application software functions using schematic maps of a target domain. Just like the map of the London Underground, the schemas usefully represent important features of the domain of application in the actual world.

The schema is the specification for the information in the database. The standard approach today is to structure information into tables in a relational database. Each table represents a type of entity or event, each row in the table represents a particular instance of that entity or event, and the columns specify each of the attributes. Permissible values for each attribute are drawn from a domain of values. For example, in a table containing financial information, there is likely to be an attribute labelled *currency*, the values for which might be drawn from a list of valid currencies published by a reliable source such as the International Standards Organisation. Most database schemas map only a very restricted domain, but there is really no limit to the scope of a database except time and resources. Every actual database can be thought of as a fragment of an imagined universal database, a database that could be loaded with a description of every entity in the universe and every event that will ever happen.

Because models are abstractions there can always be multiple models of the same domain, and the application of one model doesn't exclude the application of alternative models. The flexibility of modelling and the ability of multiple models to represent reality frees us from the rigidity of thinking that we are somehow trying to represent *the* real world. This does not imply any form of postmodern scepticism about the reality of the world or advocacy of social constructionism. The relationship between similarity and difference is not vague or subjective. Abstraction and analogy are disciplined ways of thinking, but they don't lend themselves to unequivocal conclusions. We can say that there are many models but not any models.

I see modelling as a means of avoiding imposing our definitions on the world, of getting sucked into the assumption that there is only one level of explanation. Does this mean that there is no possibility of objective knowledge? Is every application of a concept just an interpretation? This point is often misunderstood. It means that there are many truths, not a single truth. The distinction between the map and the territory is a statement of doubt, and this kind of analysis leads to this kind of doubt. It is not scepticism about knowledge as such, but scepticism about the fit between concept and actuality. The idea that there are many maps is an idea about the impossibility of unequivocal and complete knowledge, rather than the impossibility of objective knowledge. Explanation as the application of theoretical models creates the space – the necessary detachment – between the conceptual and the actual that prevents us from confusing map and terrain and allows us to see both as having their proper autonomy.

This approach implies that there are basically two kinds of statements that can be made. The first kind may be called classification statements. These describe both the structure of a conceptual model and the relationship between different conceptual models. They are 'relations of ideas', as David Hume called them. We use words to elaborate conceptual models. Sentences in the form *houses are buildings* are an example. This sentence tells us both that the type *house* inherits from the type *building* and that the population of houses is a sub-population of the population of buildings. This kind of sentence doesn't really apply to anything outside the model; it is not tethered to any ground, so to speak. Rather, it elaborates the relationship between two concepts, in this case the concepts *house* and *building*. To be semantically valid a statement must articulate the underlying conceptual data model. This data model is unlikely to be defined anywhere. When we learn a language, we intuitively pick up the underlying models and it can often require considerable careful analysis to understand these structures.

An ethical judgement such as *lying is wrong* has the same underlying structure as the sentence *houses are buildings*. It is asserting that the type *lie* inherits from the type *wrongful action* and the global population of lies is a sub-population of the global population of wrongful actions. In this case the attribute that is being inherited is *fraudulent*. Lying is fraudulent speech and fraudulence is one of the attributes that makes an action morally wrong.

The second kind of sentence can be called existential statements. These are sentences that describe a terrain through the application of one or more conceptual models. For example, when the film critic Roger Ebert writes with regard to Fellini's *La Dolce Vita* that *'he never made a more "Felliniesque" film, or a better one'*, this is an existential statement that deploys two conceptual models, the 'archetypal Fellini film' and 'the best Fellini film'. It asserts that the attributes of *La Dolce Vita* most closely match the attributes of the archetypal Fellini film and the attributes of the best Fellini film. It's left unresolved by the sentence as to whether these are the same attributes in both cases.

The domain of application may be actual events and entities, or imagined ones. The domain of application of a conceptual model may also be another conceptual model, so that the model is functioning as a meta-schema. A schema specifies the structure of a conceptual model, and a meta-schema specifies the structure of the structure.

In its most general form in English, the existential statement is *there is something*, and the remainder of the sentence describes the type of entity or event that the something is and specifies its attributes and values. Although not every existential sentence has this form, every existential sentence could be translated into this form if we wanted to. For example, the sentence *I doubt that Fellini ever made a better film than La Dolce Vita* could be restructured to the form *there is a doubt…*, with the remainder of the sentence describing whose doubt it is (mine) and what it concerns (Fellini's film-making).

The truth or falsehood of an existential statement lies in successfully completing a mapping between a conceptual model and a target set of events and entities such that they can be said to be within the model's domain of application. We are now entering somewhat treacherous territory. Are we going to lose contact with the idea of an independent reality and the possibility of truth? I don't think so. The reason is that a conceptual model permits multiple states of the target system because each attribute will take multiple values. The model for a simple switch, for example, supports two states because the attribute in the model *switch-state* has two values: on and off. The truth of an existential statement that applies this model therefore has two components: firstly, does the conceptual model map to the target system, and, secondly, is the state of the target system the state claimed in the statement?

It could be argued that classification statements are a special case of existential statements. We could, for instance, recast the sentence *houses are buildings* in the form *there is a conceptual model in which…*, but this would miss an important distinction, which is that conceptual models are constructions, human artefacts. This means that while the successful application of conceptual models requires discovery, there is an element of invention and imagination in the construction of the models. The test of a good conceptual model is not just whether it is coherent, but also whether it is usefully applicable.

This doesn't mean they are arbitrary. Conceptual structures have load-bearing components just as actual buildings and bridges do. The image I want to convey is of conceptual structures as pieces of engineering. A classification statement can be verified by examining the conceptual schema, and if the specification for one entity such as *building* is contained within the specification for another entity such as *house*, it is necessarily true that if we can apply the concept *house* to an object, we can know that the concept *building* also applies to it. The truth or falsehood of a classification statement lies in the coherence of the model. Houses are not arbitrarily buildings. If the structure of the concept *house* doesn't contain the attributes and values of the concept *building*, then the statement *houses are buildings* will be false.

An arithmetic statement such as 12÷3 = 4 is another kind of classification. It is a statement about populations. It says that if you take any population of 12 and separate it into 3 equal populations, each of those populations will be a population of 4. What distinguishes this kind of statement is the level of abstraction. Mathematics abstracts away from any actual population so that it can be applied generally to all populations, including every conceptual population and every actual population of entities and events, whatever their kind and however they are related.

The statement 12÷3 = 4 is an illustration of the conceptual model *number* rather than being itself a model, and what is being illustrated is the implications of the sequencing of numbers. There is a fixed relationship between all numbers inherent in the construction of the sequence of numbers through increments of one. For example, 3 + 4 = 7 is true because 3 is shorthand for 1+1+1; 4 is shorthand for 1+1+1+1; and 7 is shorthand for 1+1+1+1+1+1+1; and, therefore, the tally of marks to the left of the equation is the same as the tally of marks to the right.

It follows from this that there is also a fixed relationship between the components of every arithmetic operation. If the conceptual model *numbers* is applicable to a target domain, it means that the fixed relationship inherent in the concept of number will also apply to the domain of application. So, for example, because there is a fixed relationship between the components of a division statement, if we have a population and we know the size of the population and the number of divisions then we can confidently infer the population in each of the divisions.

In order that a quantified schema can be applied, the domain of application must be a population of countable or measurable entities and events of the right kind. This is what distinguishes mathematics from physics. Richard Feynman makes this point in his lectures. Physics can look like a set of interlocking equations, but $F = ma$, force = mass x acceleration, for example, is not a conceptual truth or a definition. If a mass were observed to accelerate without there being at least one other discernible mass in the neighbourhood acting as the source of the force, the conclusion would be that the model wasn't applicable and the statement wouldn't be true.

The universe is not the domain of application of mathematics. Some applications are precise; for example, the inverse square rule that describes how gravitational and electromagnetic forces vary with distance. However, most of the mathematical models deployed in the sciences are ultimately good enough approximations rather than exact applications.

Neither classification statements nor existential statements are foundational. The meaning and truth of existential statements depends on the classificatory structure by which they are framed, but it isn't sufficient for a classificatory structure to be well formed and consistent. It must also support meaningful and true existential statements. There is what Wilhelm Dilthey called a *'hermeneutic circle'*, in which conceptual structures and existential observations adapt and adjust and accommodate to each other.

Again, the possible errors that can be made in this regard can be understood as polarities. At one extreme is the idea that there are existential statements that can be made independently of any conceptual structure. At the other is the idea that existential statements are inevitably determined by the conceptual structures within which they are framed. This polarisation is unnecessary. The trick is to think in terms of many independent conceptual structures at different levels. For example, we can always test a model of scientific explanation against a general-purpose model of observation, not because the model of observation is conceptually undetermined, but because it is independent of the scientific model.

The positive case for interpretation is that it makes us aware of the abstract and partial characteristics of the way that we think. Having multiple maps makes interpretation more onerous, but at the same time frees us from dependence on a single map and prevents us from confusing the artefacts of map-making with the features of the terrain. We can keep open the possibility of making a genuine discovery about the territory.

Maps must map, and there is therefore an underlying constraint. Analogy and abstraction can stretch a long way, which is where their power comes from, but not every way or any way. The map of the London Underground is a very abstract, very schematic, representation of the services; a construct. But it is only useful because there is a mapping between the symbols on the map and some features of the terrain to which it is applied.

When this works successfully, inferences can be drawn from the application of conceptual models. Because of the density of our conceptual architecture it is often possible to make far-reaching inferences from just a few touch points. We recognise this with successful models: a complex map might apply to a complex terrain and a simplified map to a simplified terrain, but what we are looking for are maps that with an economy of means have an extensive domain of application.

This model of truth isn't unequivocal in the way that the binary idea that statements are either true or false suggests. But it is not really so different. The binary idea of truth asserts that there is a single truth and an infinite number of errors. This model asserts that there are a relatively small number of applicable models and an infinite number of inapplicable models; that applicability is a graduated dimension and that, much of the time, that gradient is a steep one.

CHAPTER THREE

# ASYMMETRY AND SCALE

## The physicists' argument

It is a question of scale. In physics there are two different models that describe how nature works, one for the small scale and one for the large scale. Quantum theory describes nature at the micro-scale of nuclear forces and electromagnetism while general relativity theory describes nature at the macro-scale of gravity. General relativity cannot be scaled down to the micro-scale and quantum theory cannot be scaled up to the macro-scale.

The science journalist Corey Powell describes these as two separate rulebooks explaining how nature works. General relativity can be applied to planets and galaxies and the dynamics of the expanding universe, and quantum theory can describe what happens when a uranium atom decays or when particles of light hit a solar cell, but:

> *Now for the problem: relativity and quantum mechanics are fundamentally different theories that have different*

> *formulations. It is not just a matter of scientific terminology; it is a clash of genuinely incompatible descriptions of reality.*

As Powell describes it, there are a number of dimensions to this incompatibility. In general relativity the evolution of a system is continuous and deterministic and interactions are localised. 'Continuous' means that transitions between states are smooth, such that between any two states of a system there are an infinite number of intermediate states; 'deterministic' means that there is an invariable succession of events; and 'localised' means that the influence of one event on another event is constrained by the speed at which information can be disseminated, which is ultimately the speed of light. General relativity allows no place for an outside observer or an external clock, because there is no outside. Instead, all of reality is described in terms of relationships between objects and between different regions of space.

In quantum theory, on the other hand, the evolution of a system is discontinuous and probabilistic, and it may be that interactions are not always localised. There are a finite number of discrete states that a system can be in, and transitions between states happen in jumps, so-called quantum leaps, with no intermediate state possible; instead of an invariable succession of events there is a probabilistic succession of events; and it seems to be the case that systems can remain entangled even though it appears impossible that any information could be passing between them. Powell remarks that quantum theory discards our familiar notions about space and locality.

Powell's essay reviews the work of some of the theorists who are trying to find solutions to the problem. Taking a larger view, the real issue is not general relativity versus quantum field theory, but classical dynamics versus quantum dynamics. Relativity, despite its perceived strangeness, is in this sense classical, while quantum mechanics is not. Although Einstein was optimistic that some deeper discoveries would uncover a classical, deterministic reality hiding beneath quantum mechanics, no such order has yet been found.

Powell suggests that most physicists share a core conviction that general relativity will ultimately prove subordinate to quantum theory. The other three fundamental forces of physics follow quantum rules, so doesn't it make sense that gravity must as well?

There is also a philosophical commitment. The suggestion is that the majority of physicists regard the large-scale reality of classical physics as a kind of illusion, an approximation that emerges from the truer aspects of the quantum world operating at an extremely small scale. But not everyone subscribes to this consensus. A different approach is taken by scientists such as Lee Smolin, a critic of string theory:

> *Smolin thinks the small-scale approach to physics is inherently incomplete. Current versions of quantum field theory do a fine job explaining how individual particles or small systems of particles behave, but they fail to take into account what is needed to have a sensible theory of the*

> *cosmos as a whole. They don't explain why reality is like this, and not like something else.*

Answering this question requires us to consider the universe as a single system and to build a new kind of theory that can apply to the whole thing. The advantage of general relatively is that it already provides a framework for that approach.

One question Powell doesn't ask but which also reflects a deep philosophical commitment in modern science is whether it might turn out that quantum mechanics and general relativity, rather than being two incomplete and partial theories that will one day be unified, are in fact two complete models that are applicable at different scales.

As Powell suggest, it is not sufficient just to get the two classes of physics theories to work together in a putative theory of everything. The further question is why the universe is the way it is and not something else. How did we end up with this universe and these regularities and orderings and not another one? String theory has recently been the dominant attempt to create a unified model of physics. One of the criticisms of string theory is that it allows so many possible universes that it can't really explain why this universe is the way it is except for concluding that if it wasn't this way then we wouldn't be here to ask the question. In string theory there are so many possible universes that some universes inevitably look like this one.

Quantum theory cannot be scaled up to explain why the universe looks like this and not like something else. Furthermore, there is a more pressing difficulty with the idea that the macro-scale is some kind of illusion:

> *No matter how the theories shake out, the large scale is inescapably important, because it is the world we inhabit and observe. In essence, the universe as a whole is the answer... there is an entire cosmos out there with unique properties that need to be explained – something that, for now at least, quantum physics alone cannot do.*
>
> *The best thing it* [a future theory] *can do is create deeper meaning that connects back to us the observers.*

Whatever direction the future development of physics takes, it will need to contribute a solution to one of the basic problems of modern science, which is how to connect scientific theory to our experience of existence as human beings.

# The scientific picture

In current thinking about the meaning of science, the prevailing framework of ideas is philosophical naturalism. The term 'naturalism' is imprecise, and can be claimed for different and contradictory ideas, but a useful starting point might be something like the following, from Peter Godfrey-Smith in his book *Theory and Reality*:

> *Naturalism holds that we can only hope to resolve philosophical problems (including epistemological problems) by approaching them within a scientific picture of ourselves and our place in the universe.*

Naturalism is the idea that science itself functions as a framework within which to approach philosophical questions. This is an anti-foundationalist approach to thinking about science grounded in the idea of the autonomy of science. Instead of trying to build a philosophical foundation for science in the way that the logical positivists tried and failed to do in the first half of the 20th century, Godfrey-Smith suggests that the distinctive feature of naturalism is the absence of foundations. Instead, science is best thought of as what the scientific community does, and the scientific enterprise as one that evolves through time.

Traditionally, the principal concerns of philosophical thinking are epistemological, ethical, and metaphysical. In Kant's formulation, we can say that philosophical thinking is concerned with three questions: what we can know; what we should do; and what we might hope for; the last because what we might hope for is dependent on the nature of ultimate reality. One of the difficulties with basing our thinking about these questions on the scientific picture is that natural science has only a limited scope: broadly, the events described in physics, chemistry and biology. Much of the familiar world we inhabit is outside the domain of application of modern science. So how then do the disciplines of science contribute to a response to these questions? How do we find there the *deeper meaning that connects back to us, the observers?*

The possibilities of philosophical naturalism are constrained not only by the limitations of modern science, but also because the ramifications of scientific thinking require interpretation. What is implied by a scientific description if the scientific picture can be interpreted both as an abstract mathematical model and as a description of the actual world? There are at least three alternative answers to this question, which might be called positivism, reductivism and essentialism.

Positivism avoids metaphysics as much as possible. From this perspective we should see science as one among many abstract representations of reality, convenient for some purposes but not for others. In *A Brief History of Time*, Stephen Hawking gives a description of the fundamental interactions of particle physics which draws attention to the artifice of the model. The important words in Hawking's description that identify it as a positivist perspective are *'supposed to be'*, *'just as if'* and *'convenient for'*:

> *All the known particles in the universe can be divided into two groups: particles of spin ½, which make up the matter in the universe, and particles of spin 0, 1 and 2, which give rise to forces between the matter particles.*
>
> *In quantum mechanics, the forces of interactions between matter particles are all supposed to be carried by particles of integer spin – 0, 1 or 2. What happens is that a matter particle, such as an electron or quark, emits a force carrying particle. The recoil from this emission changes the velocity of the matter particle. The force carrying particle then collides with another matter particle and is absorbed. This collision changes the velocity of the second particle, just as if there had been a force between the two matter particles.*
>
> *Force carrying particles can be grouped into four categories according to the strength of the force that they carry and the particles with which they interact. It should be emphasized that this division into four classes is man-made: it is convenient for the construction of partial theories, but it may not correspond to anything deeper.*

Reductivism and essentialism, on the other hand, are metaphysical positions. Both are grounded in the idea that the events described by science are descriptions of real events rather than being features of an abstract model of the observable world. The realist interpretation of science is that the events postulated by science are continuous with the familiar observable world. The difference between the two positions is that the reductivist believes that events and entities at the micro-scale of particle physics are the basic reality, while the essentialist believes that the events and entities at the macro-scale of human experience are the basic reality.

The difference in perspective between positivism and reductivism arises because the objects and events postulated by physics don't have a separate existence in the observable world, an existence independent of the scientific model. What happens is that, first, an abstract model is built to explain the observable world, and then this model is used to postulate the existence of unobservable objects such as bosons, leptons and quarks. Reductivism is the result when the objects and events arrived at by this double movement of abstraction and projection are taken to be in some way the underlying or basic reality of the world.

The philosopher Wilfred Sellars provided an argument for this position that explains why it is based on a model of composition. In his essay *Philosophy and the Scientific Image of Man,* Sellars suggested we have two images of the world, the scientific image and the manifest image:

> *The scientific image…is, of course, as much an idealization as the manifest image – even more so, as it is still in the process of coming to be. It will be remembered that the contrast I have in mind is not that between an unscientific conception… and a scientific one, but between that conception which limits itself to what correlational techniques can tell us about perceptible and introspectable events and that which*

> *postulates imperceptible objects and events for the purpose of explaining correlations among perceptibles.*

In other words, the manifest image is a model that explains the observable in terms of the observable, whereas the scientific image is a model that postulates the unobservable in order to explain the observable.

Reductivism shouldn't be confused with arguments about whether or not a whole can be more than the sum of its parts. As Sellars explains, we need to draw a distinction between composition in the sense in which the frame and the rungs are the parts of a ladder, and composition in the sense in which an ice cube is constituted by water molecules.

In the case of the ladder, the components are heterogeneous and the ladder as a whole and the rungs and the frame taken separately have their own proper attributes. A ladder is what I have been calling a modular structure. In the case of the ice cubes, the components are homogeneous; the attributes of the stuff, the ice cube, are the attributes of its constituents, the water molecules. In this view, science is concerned with constitutive stuff, what I have called cellular structures, rather than with modular wholes:

> *If an object is in a strict sense a system of objects, then every property of the object must consist in the fact that its constituents have such and such qualities and stand in such and such relations or, roughly, every property of a system of*

*objects consists of properties of, and relations between, its constituents.*

*With something like this principle in mind, it was argued that if a physical object is in a strict sense a system of imperceptible particles, then it cannot as a whole have the perceptible qualities characteristic of physical objects in the manifest image. It was concluded that manifest physical objects are 'appearances' to human perceivers of systems of imperceptible particles...*

This approach to the interpretation of science excludes from the basic reality much of the furniture of familiar experience, including meaning, value and purpose, as these are attributes of entities and events in the manifest image. This is inevitable as things stand, because meaning, value and purpose are not concepts in modern science. The way this is usually described is to say that the macro-scale structures of the observable world that carry meaning, value and purpose supervene on the meaningless micro-scale structures described by modern physics.

My suggestion with regards to classification is that scientific materialism is a version of reductivism rather than another term for the same thing. There are a couple of reasons for this. The first is that scientific materialism isn't the only interpretation of science possible within the framework of reductivism. Interpretation can go in entirely different directions: towards panpsychism; towards the natural teleology advocated by Thomas Nagel in his book

*Mind and Cosmos*; or towards what might be called, without any intention to disparage it, mystical reductivism.

The terminology here is not settled. To avoid confusion, I am following Nagel's terminology. Nagel uses *reductive* as the general term for theories that analyse the properties of complex wholes into the properties of their most basic elements, and *reductionist* for the more specific types of theory that analyse macro-scale phenomena exclusively in terms of their physical properties.

This means that it is possible to have an idealist reductivism. Nagel's argument is anti-materialist rather than anti-reductivist. He describes his position as, in a broad sense, idealist in the tradition of Plato:

> *It seems to me that one cannot really understand the scientific world view unless one assumes that the intelligibility of the world…is itself part of the deepest explanation of why things are as they are. So, when we prefer one explanation of the same data to another because it is simpler and makes fewer arbitrary assumptions… it is because we think the explanation that gives greater understanding is more likely to be true, just for that reason… This assumption is a form of the principle of sufficient reason.*

Nagel's is an idealist reductivism, whereas mainstream thinking is materialist reductivism. However, while the labels 'materialist' and 'idealist' are convenient and come from the philosophical tradition, materialism isn't really very well defined. Matter lacks definition in science. The underlying insight is called 'neutral monism', and goes back to the 19th century and the work of Ernst Mach. It is based on the principle of keeping things simple. This is how Peter Godfrey-Smith articulates it, in a review of Nagel's book:

> It [neutral monism] *holds that standard ways of thinking about the mind–body problem are dependent on crude conceptions of both the mental and the physical. We think we have a clear and definite idea of what a 'purely physical' or 'purely mental' process is like, but our grasp of both is so poor that we do a bad job of thinking about how they might be related, and see a gulf that isn't really there.*

The real force behind the distinction between materialism and idealism is whether you believe the order in the world is ultimately accidental, or ultimately the expression of some kind of necessity. Nagel continues:

> *The view that rational intelligibility is the root of the natural order makes me, in a broad sense, an idealist... [T]he intelligibility of the world is no accident... I suspect that there must be a strain of this kind of idealism in every theoretical scientist: pure empiricism is not enough.*

Reductivism tends to accompany a secular sensibility, but a version compatible with a religious sensibility is also possible. What I am calling 'mystical reductivism' accepts that physics describes the basic reality and is therefore more than a model, but reasons from this that therefore meaning, value and purpose must also, in some way we don't yet understand, inform the basic structures of the universe. This view has been articulated by Freeman Dyson, writing in the *New York Review of Books*, though I think he would call it Platonism rather than mysticism:

> *I am a practicing Christian but not a believing Christian. To me, to worship God means to recognize that mind and intelligence are woven into the fabric of our universe in a way that altogether surpasses our comprehension.*

The disadvantage of idealist and mystical versions of reductivism is that it is difficult to explain in any detail how they might actually work, but they do have the advantage of coherence with the underlying assumption of reductivism, a coherence that scientific materialism lacks. The argument is this: if the logic of reductivism is correct and every event in the universe is determined at the micro-scale, *and* there is meaning, value and purpose in the universe, then it must also follow that meaning, value and purpose are being determined at the micro-scale in some way that panpsychism, natural teleology and mystical reductivism are attempting to intuit.

The problem with scientific materialism is therefore the converse: if everything is determined at the micro-scale and the micro-scale lacks meaning, value and purpose, then it is difficult to see how these properties can occur at any other scale. Leibniz' solution is one possibility. Leibniz invoked providential harmony as the reason for the existence of meaningful structures sustainable at the scale of familiar experience. God binds together the micro-scale and the macro-scale – or perhaps we might say that the force required to bind the macro to the micro is the thing we call 'God'. Scientific materialism looks to biological evolution rather than providence to solve the problem, but as evolution is a macro-scale process, it isn't obvious that this is a valid solution within the terms of the hypothesis.

Wilfred Sellars' own preferred solution is what might be thought of as the horizontal extension of science:

> *Thus, to complete the scientific image we need to enrich it not with more ways of saying what is the case, but with the language of community and individual intentions, so that by construing the actions we intend to do and the circumstances in which we intend to do them in scientific terms, we directly relate the world as conceived by scientific theory to our purposes, and make it our world and no longer an alien appendage to the world in which we do our living. We can, of course, as matters now stand, realize this direct incorporation of the scientific image into our way of life only in imagination. But to do so is, if only in imagination, to transcend the dualism of the manifest and scientific images.*

The second justification for using the term reductivism for this family of ideas is that it allows for a clear contrast with essentialism. By essentialism I mean the idea that the entities and events of familiar observable experience are the basic reality, or in some way correlated with the prototypes or archetypes that are the basic reality. Essentialism might also be called holistic compositionalism. In the reductive interpretation of compositionalism, familiar objects can be explained as the outcome of events at the micro-scale; macro-scale objects are transient vehicles that are brought into existence as a consequence of the adventures of micro-scale components. In the holistic interpretation of compositionalism, the familiar objects of experience at the macro-scale are the outcome of more or less successful attempts by some force to organise the resistant materials of the micro-scale into an intelligible order.

Essentialism is grounded, not surprisingly, in the intuition of essences. The metaphysics of Plato and Aristotle were versions of essentialism, as were the scholasticisms of Thomas Aquinas and Duns Scotus. It is the pre-scientific way of thinking, and may be a naturally intuitive way for human beings to think. In modern philosophy this intuition of essences has been the underlying assumption of the phenomenological and existentialist thinking that runs in a line of descent from Hegel. When Sartre says, with regard to humanity, that existence precedes essence, he is defining humanity's freedom from pre-definition as an exception. However, Sartre's thinking still retains the essentialist framework, which takes human beings and all the other objects and events of familiar experience to be the fundamental units of analysis, the basic reality. This is the point Heidegger makes in his rejoinder to Sartre, that reversing the polarities isn't escaping the framework.

*Thing, being, object, entity*: we usually take these to be somewhat vague abstractions in our everyday usage. Everything is a *thing* of some kind, isn't it? But being a thing has traditionally meant more than simply existing; it has meant existing as something intelligible, where being intelligible isn't an accidental attribute. To exist, for Heidegger, at least in his earlier work, means to be something usable, to be a piece of equipment, always already something ready-to-hand. To be merely there, present-at-hand, is to be broken and useless, a distinction that is a concrete expression of this idea that intelligibility isn't accidental. Similarly, for Sartre, being means existing as a thing, to have definition as a thing. For this reason, although essentialism may point in an idealist or mystical direction, there can't really be a materialist essentialism, as this would imply entities and events were shaped by an accidental necessity.

Existence isn't here problematic. There is something if there is anything, and if there is anything there is everything. If there is something, then every event is a transformation of that something, and the question can then become why it takes the form we observe here and now. We can ask, why does anything exist and not nothing? Is it somehow easier for there to be something rather than nothing? It's a sensible question but it's not clear how you might even begin to answer it.

On the other hand, it doesn't make sense to ask why a particular tree or a particular building exists as if it comes from nowhere. Particular things don't come into being independently, they are transformations of the whole that already exists into a particular configuration at a particular location. So, once you have crossed the boundary from non-existence to existence, whatever form it takes, the existence of anything and therefore of everything ceases to be problematic. What is in question is why it take this form and not some other form.

In the same way Heidegger's critique of modern science in *The Question Concerning Technology* is that it dissolves the familiar objects of experience into objectlessness, by which he also means *no-thing-ness*. This objectlessness is usually translated in English as 'standing-reserve', a translation that unfortunately loses the force of the opposition of the German terms that lies behind Heidegger's point: *Gegenstand*, literally 'standing against', meaning 'object' and *Bestande* meaning 'stuff'. Heidegger makes the same argument about finance. To the finance director, things of all kinds – whether people, equipment or ideas – are all just assets and liabilities on the balance sheet, and are all therefore substitutable. Their distinctiveness as things is dissolved in the homogeneous category of accounting entry.

This intuition of essences has also been revived recently within the tradition of philosophical naturalism, notably by Saul Kripke. In Kripke's view, science tries to find better descriptions of natural kinds. The idea is that natural kinds are real in some way that artificial kinds, which are clearly the product of human interventions, are not. For Kripke, natural kinds are the entities and events of familiar experience: tigers, heat, gold, water and so on, and according to this view the goal of science is to find better descriptions for these entities and events of the familiar world. This is how Kripke puts it in *Naming & Necessity*:

> *In general, science attempts, by investigating basic structural traits, to find the nature, and thus the essence (in the philosophical sense), of the kind.*

This implies that natural kinds are the basic reality and remain constant through time. What changes in scientific progress are the conceptual models used to give an account of the nature of each kind and, from this perspective, it is the events and entities of the macro-scale that are the basic reality and the units of analysis for science. Because the unit of analysis doesn't change, there is the further implication that a complete and accurate description is, at least potentially, attainable.

In both its classical and modern forms essentialism is a movement from logic to metaphysics, a movement that, in my view, goes in the wrong direction. Classically, essentialism starts with the logical requirements for definition and the distinction between necessary and accidental properties that this implies, and then proposes that these types map to something that is metaphysically real; an implicit assumption that the necessities of our own logic inhere in the fabric of the universe. Right at the beginning of Western philosophy, Plato took the definitions that Socrates sought to use in argument to counter his opponents, the Sophists, and turned them into *Ideas*, real although transcendent entities and events that serve as the models for entities and events in the observable world.

In modern philosophical thinking the approach is more likely to start from the modal logic of necessity and possibility, but the movement is the same. The move can be observed in the assertion that water is $H_2O$. The assertion occurs in the context of an argument about definitions and identities. The argument is that although this is an identity, where being an identity means that it holds in all possible worlds, it is also an empirical discovery about the world that water has the molecular composition represented by $H_2O$ and, if this is the case, the implication is that definitions are not only logical structures but also facts about the world. If this case can be made, the naturalistic world view that everything is susceptible to scientific explanation might be given a foundation.

The problem with the argument is that when we say a sample of water is also a sample of $H_2O$, we are not giving a definition or stating an identity; rather we are drawing attention to the interesting fact that in this case there is a simple one-to-one mapping between the manifest image and the scientific image of the world. It is a bridging statement between two different conceptual structures. That you can do this, more or less, with water and some other stuffs such as salt is happenstance, something that can be seen by thinking about earth and air and fire, the other elements in pre-scientific thinking, which have no simple one-to-one mapping to entities in the scientific image. Earth and air are aggregates, and fire is the visible evidence of an event, the process of heating oxygen.

These arguments might seem to be applying unnecessary weight which the sciences were not constructed to bear. Why not simply stop at the positivism that Hawking advocates? The problem is that in practice such restraint isn't sustainable. The motivation

Sellars attributes to philosophers applies to all of us; we are all at some level trying to understand *'how things in the broadest possible sense… hang together'*; and if science holds only so far, buckling when additional interpretative pressure is applied, this is an argument for moving beyond it, not for simply accepting that the explanations science can provide are all there is to say on the matter.

Stephen Hawking himself, for example, although advocating a positivist approach, has argued for determinism and against the possibility of free will, an argument that depends on a metaphysical stance; and there are also remarks in *A Brief History of Time* about understanding the mind of God that suggest he also shared something of Dyson's mysticism.

## Statistical and mechanical order

Erwin Schrödinger was one of the founders of quantum theory and was awarded the Nobel Prize for Physics in 1933. Later in his career he wrote a couple of essays for a non-specialist audience on the topic of the physics and chemistry of life and the physics and chemistry of the mind. In the first, *What Is Life?*, which was published in 1944, Schrödinger is concerned with questions of scale, stability, composition and order:

> *How can the events in space and time which take place within the spatial boundary of a living organism be accounted for by physics and chemistry?*

The DNA molecule had been identified in 1869, but it wouldn't be until 1952, eight years after Schrödinger was writing, that its role in heredity was confirmed, and 1953 before the shape of its double helix structure was discovered. Schrödinger was theorising from what was then known when he speculated as to what the coding mechanism for inheritance would have to be.

> *The preliminary answer which this little book will endeavour to expound and establish can be summarized as follows: The obvious inability of present-day physics and chemistry to account for such events is no reason at all for doubting that they can be accounted for by those sciences.*

However, in order for this to happen, Schrödinger believed that explaining life would require a new set of principles. This is because the construction of living systems is different from the construction of non-living systems. The difference Schrödinger has in mind is between statistically ordered systems and mechanically ordered systems, or what he calls order-from-disorder and order-from-order.

What does Schrödinger mean by order-from-disorder? Much of the regularity described by physics and chemistry is a statistical regularity. The order and predictability comes from the aggregation of the behaviour of very large populations rather than from the behaviour of a small number of components. Statistical order implies a probabilistic pattern of succession of events. He gives a number of examples drawn from statistical mechanics, the science of thermodynamics. The first example concerns magnetisation. If you place a container filled with oxygen in a magnetic field, the oxygen molecules will align with the field. But not all of them. We know this because when you double the strength of the field you double the magnetisation of the oxygen, implying that more of the molecules are aligned. The reason is that the magnetisation effect is in conflict with the background turbulence in the system that is acting to randomise the orientation of the molecules. At the micro-scale individual molecules change orientation constantly, but the small preponderance generated by the magnet, when averaged over the total population, generates a statistically predictable magnetisation of the whole system.

Brownian motion is similar. Again, if you were to fill a container with a fog of water droplets, the level of the fog would sink at a predictable rate under the effect of gravity. However, if you looked at the motion of an individual droplet it would show an irregular movement. This is because the droplets are sufficiently small for their path to be influenced by the impact of single molecules. It is only at the aggregate level that the sinking becomes reliable and predictable.

A similar effect occurs with attempts to measure forces such as electromagnetism by suspending a light body on a very thin filament as a torsional balance. There is a limit to the practicality of this method, which is reached when the filament and the body become susceptible to the impact of the surrounding molecules and start to perform an irregular dance, making single observations unreliable. To counter this, multiple observations have to be made to eliminate the effect of the Brownian motion.

Schrödinger's third example is diffusion. Imagine a container filled with water, with a small amount of another substance such as potassium permanganate dissolved in it such that the concentration diminishes from the left to right of the container. Over time, left to itself, the concentration of the permanganate will equalise until it is evenly distributed in the container. But each molecule of the permanganate behaves independently and follows a random walk. How is it that a random walk at the scale of an individual molecule is a mathematically predictable process at the scale of the population as a whole? The way to see this is to imagine the container cut by a series of vertical planes. Although there is an equal probability that a single molecule will be carried to the left or to the right of a plane, while there are more molecules to the left than to the right of each plane, the probability is that more molecules will cross from left to right than from right to left. In this way the concentration will even out.

If we abstract from these specific examples, we can ask a general question. Why do we have to use statistics to understand the order in some systems, and what kind of systems are these? A couple of ideas come to mind. The first is the situation in which there are a set of possible configurations and no particular bias favouring any particular one. This is the basis of chance, and underlies gambling games with cards, dice or the randomness of flipping a coin. This kind of system is exemplified by the example of the diffusion of potassium permanganate in a container of water.

The second kind of system is suggested by the examples of Brownian motion and magnetism. These are systems were there are multiple factors influencing the behaviour of the system and pulling in different directions. You need a statistical analysis because it is necessary to eliminate the effect of competing influences and the background noise caused by randomness in the system.

Schrödinger writes that there are thousands of such examples of this phenomenon in physics. The level of inaccuracy to be expected in any physical relation can be quantified as $\sqrt{n}$, where $n$ is the number of molecules in the population. Because it is a square root, the margin of error relative to the size of the population under consideration decreases the larger the population becomes. The $\sqrt{100} = 10$, therefore with 100 molecules in the sample the relative error will be 10%; the $\sqrt{1,000,000}$ is 1,000, and so for the larger population the relative error will be only 0.1%.

By order-from-order Schrödinger means mechanical processes that follow an invariable pattern of succession. The paradigm example is clockwork. The movement of the planets is also an example of order-from-order. Schrödinger's argument is that the fundamental order of the universe is statistical, even though many systems appear to be mechanical at the macro-scale. The transition is dependent on temperature. All systems are mechanical at absolute zero, and statistical at some level of temperature. For example, at room temperature a pendulum is at the equivalent of absolute zero: it will continue to function as a pendulum however much further the system is cooled, but if it is heated the pendulum will eventually melt and then vaporise.

In Schrödinger's argument, how does order-from-order persist in a system where the underlying pattern is order-from-disorder? Something must happen at the macro-scale to neutralise the effects of the micro-scale disorder. The reason is that mechanical processes come about because larger scale bodies are bound by forces that are strong enough to overcome the underlying disorder. The disorderly state is fundamental, but there are islands of stability in the ocean of turbulence.

This stability is highly dependent on temperature. The underlying insight of quantum theory is that, at a very small scale, the world is discrete rather than continuous. This means there are a limited number of possible configurations of any system. For this reason, the atoms in a molecule can normally only adopt one of a limited number of discrete configurations. The general rule with molecules is that they are isomeric, that is, the same set of atoms can occur in multiple stable configurations at different levels and with different properties.

Each configuration is stable and there are no spontaneous transitions between them. The reason for this absence of transitions is that these configurations are not neighbours. To transition between the configurations, the system would have to pass through an intermediate state that is at a higher level than either of the two stable configurations. The intermediate state functions as a threshold, in the same sense that to get from one valley to the next you have to climb the mountain that separates them.

One dimension of these configurations is energy level. Systems can spontaneously transition to a state at a lower energy level with the surplus energy spent as radiation, but they require an external energy source to lift the system to a configuration at a higher energy level. This creates partitioned systems, where the partitioning is due to the presence of thresholds:

> *We must content ourselves with examining the point which is of paramount interest for our biological question, namely, the stability of a molecule at different temperatures… To lift it to the next higher state or level a definite supply of energy is required. The simplest way of trying to supply it is to 'heat up' your molecule. You bring it into an environment of*

> *higher temperature ('heat bath'), thus allowing other systems (atoms, molecules) to impinge upon it. Considering the entire irregularity of heat motion, there is no sharp temperature limit at which the 'lift' will be brought about with certainty and immediately. Rather at any temperature (different from absolute zero) there is a certain smaller or greater chance for the lift to occur, the chance increasing of course with the temperature of the heat bath. The best way to express this chance is to indicate the average time you will have to wait until the lift takes place, the 'time of expectation'.*

What happens when an external energy source is applied and a molecular system is heated up? Because heating is irregular, there isn't a definite time limit at which the lift to a higher state occurs, but the more heat that is applied, the higher becomes the probability that such a lift will occur. The average time it will take to effect a lift depends on the scale of the lift relative to average heat energy. This is an exponential function that is a measure of the improbability of an amount of energy sufficiently large gathering accidently in some part of the system. Because it is an exponential function, this improbability increases enormously when a considerable multiple of the average energy is required.

This dynamic looks like a point of intersection between disorder and order and therefore a point of origin for macro-scale partitioning. Molecules are stable because they are effectively solids.

Schrödinger's motive for writing his book is to argue that living matter, while not, as he puts it, eluding the established principles of physics, is likely therefore to involve new principles, because the persistence of order in living organisms is not explicable through the conceptual models of physics and chemistry.

Living organisms are the only natural systems in which a very small number of molecules evolve in the pattern order-from-order. Biological stability is grounded in chemical stability, and the stability of life is therefore built on the stability of molecules. Furthermore, if the possibility of life is dependent on the stability of molecules, then by extension the possibility of intelligence is dependent on the same stability. Because intelligence requires complexity, only a system with sufficient stability and sufficient complexity can be intelligent, and only at the scale of a complex living organism is such stability and such complexity possible.

## The biologists' argument

In his concise book *Shaping Life* the biologist John Maynard Smith suggests:

> *It is important for biologists to know some physics... because physics is the best exemplar we have of the kind of theories that can exist, and of the ways they may explain reality. But it is important for physical scientists moving into biology to be aware they are entering a strange territory, in which two unfamiliar concepts – adaptation and information – are central.*

Smith's book started life as a lecture, the purpose of which was to update non-specialists on what were then recent advances in molecular biology and their implications for the understanding of embryology and evolution. Maynard Smith places the emphasis on the unfamiliar concepts of biology, information and adaptation, and is therefore in a kind of dialogue with biologists such as Brian Goodwin, who place more emphasis on the continuity with physics. Maynard Smith and Goodwin were colleagues at the University of Sussex, and Goodwin's book *How the Leopard Changed Its Spots* was published a few years earlier. It is an interesting exercise to read the two together.

There is a persistence of order in living organisms. Biological organisms actively function to sustain themselves – they are homeostatic. Living systems are self-sustaining. They build, maintain and reproduce themselves. The development of a living organism can be thought of as a program. There is a store of information and there are inputs and outputs. In the processes of cell metabolism, the inputs, typically protein molecules, are dis-assembled and the parts used to assemble new molecular components, also usually proteins, which are then either deployed internally to build, maintain and reproduce the cell or are dispatched into the organism's transport systems as molecular outputs.

This difference between physical and biological systems can be regarded as two different kinds of performance, two different ways in which systems evolve. The examples Maynard Smith gives of physical systems are the vortices that develop when liquids drain from a tank and the way a drop of liquid creates a crown effect as it splashes on the floor. A vortex is an example of spontaneous order in the sense that there isn't a program or a set of instructions. There is no program, no memory and no continuity in these effects. Whatever it is that explains the formation of a vortex, it is not located in the water molecules or any other component of the system, and a vortex isn't self-sustaining.

The central dogma of molecular biology as formulated by Francis Crick is that DNA → RNA → proteins. This can be read to imply that it is DNA that drives the process, an interpretation that underlies gene-centric accounts of biological evolution. But in Maynard Smith's description, the central dogma is concerned more with partitioning and encapsulation than with triggers and sequences. The cell is the factory, and it is cell activity that is driving the process. The DNA molecule is a piece of the molecular machinery that functions reliably to stamp the molecular outputs of the factory into certain shapes.

Cells come from cells. One part of the theory of evolution is the idea that there is a single tree of life. As yet, there is no theoretical consensus on how cells were assembled in the first place, but the first cells are thought to have originated fairly early in the planet's history, maybe a little over a billion years after the formation of the Earth some 4.5 billion years ago.

The indispensable component in sustaining this unity is the DNA molecule, which is present in every cell. There are two aspects to this. The first is concerned with cell functioning. There is a one-to-one correspondence between the configuration of the DNA molecule and the structure of the protein molecules that are assembled in the cell. The presence of the DNA molecule in the cell means that when new molecules are assembled, they are reliably assembled in the same shape, a process Maynard Smith calls template reproduction. The second aspect is concerned with cell reproduction. Cells come from cells by division, and the daughter cells have the same information as the mother cell.

The second significant feature of living organisms is the distribution of the DNA module in every cell. A living organism is at the same time a cellular structure, a modular structure and a system. Collections of cells form a cellular structure through repetition, a modular structure through differentiation, and a system through the distribution of control to each cell. The system is decentralised in the sense that each cell operates to its own program; there is no central controller.

So, if the same machinery is present in every cell with the same instructions, why do cells function in different ways depending on where they are located spatially in the organism? Maynard Smith suggests that the picture that is emerging from development genetics is one of a hierarchy of regulatory genes. Genes can be switched on or off. In multicellular organisms, while all cells contain a complete set of genes, the actual process depends on the successive activation of different sets of genes in different places. Sets of genes are switched on or off and these settings are also transmitted to the daughter cells that are produced from the division of the original cell. The result is that development can be divided into successive processes of differentiation.

One way this happens is through a negative switch. For example, a cell might metabolise lactose, and this is done because one of the genes in the cell leads to the production of a particular molecular output that functions as an enzyme. However, the production of this enzyme is normally inhibited by the presence of protein molecules produced by another gene within the cell. These bind to the gene that produces the enzyme, inhibiting its operation. However, lactose molecules also bind to the regulatory protein, and when this happens the regulatory proteins cannot also inhibit the enzyme producing gene. In this way, in the presence of lactose molecules, the enzyme required to metabolise them is produced.

Maynard Smith notes that what is interesting about gene control is that it can be symbolic. That is, there is no necessary connection between form and function, in much the same way as there is no necessary connection between the form of a word and its meaning. This flexibility means that a finite set of components can perform an almost infinite set of functions.

However, in evolution the amount of morphological complexity that can be added in a single step is small if mistakes are to be avoided. The complex morphology of a Drosophila fly doesn't arise as a consequence of a single dynamical process affecting the whole organism, but in a series of steps, the later steps affecting only a small part of the organism. The embryo is successively divided into smaller and smaller regions, and development is to a degree autonomous in each region.

This autonomy has important consequences for evolution. For example, it explains why evolution tends to be gradual. The idea is that if there is an order such that development events A, B, C and D happen in sequence, then a variation at D is likely to have only an incremental and contained impact on the organism that develops, whereas a variation at A is likely to have an organism-wide impact. Because successful evolution usually depends on incremental change, and changes at step A are less likely to be incremental, the implication is that in successful lineages A will very probably be stable.

Maynard Smith argues that molecular biology has been very successful in explaining the development of individual organisms and some of the features of the path that evolution has taken, including the incrementalism.

Whereas the relationship between DNA molecule and the protein molecules produced in cell metabolism is one-to-one, the relationship between protein molecules and the morphology of the organism that develops is one-to-many. This is where the difference in the type of explanation is found. On the one side are biologists such as Maynard Smith who imply that the genetic code is the preponderant explanation for why life has evolved the form that it has, and on the other side are those such as Goodwin who argue that the genetic code has the more limited role of selecting and stabilising one of the available forms. Whereas Maynard Smith places most emphasis on adaptation and information, concepts that don't occur in physics and chemistry, Goodwin argues for greater continuity with physics. In this view, biological processes should be considered high probability spatial transformations, rather than improbable states that depend on a precise genetic program for their stability – or 'life on the edge of chaos', as Goodwin puts it.

This difference is a matter of emphasis rather than a question of alternative solutions. Goodwin provides three examples of what he means: the way that leaves grow on the stalk of a plant, the commonality in the way tetrapod limbs develop, and the repeated evolution of eyes in multiple lineages:

> *The main proposal is that all the main morphological characteristics of organisms – hearts, brains, guts, limbs,*

> *eyes, leaves, flowers, roots, trunks, branches…are the robust results of morphogenetic principles.*

There are about 250,000 species of flowering plant species and an unimaginable variety of forms, but despite this profusion there are only three ways in which leaves can be arranged on a stem. The name for this arrangement is phyllotaxis. Distichous phyllotaxis means that the leaves are arranged in two alternating lines on opposite sides of the stem, as with grasses; decussate phyllotaxis means the leaves are arranged in a whorl like a fuchsia; and spiral phyllotaxis means that each leaf is arranged in sequence above the last but offset at a fixed angle, typically 137.5 degrees, as in a yucca. Goodwin's suggestion is that these are three modes of a single engine and are due to how well the cells resist pressures generated in the underlying tissue:

Goodwin's second example is the limbs of tetrapods that, despite all the differences between amphibians, reptiles, birds and mammals, are all basically the same form. This commonality of form was recognised in the 18th century, and at that time tended to be interpreted in Platonic terms as the consequence of the unity of an archetype manifesting itself in different forms according to practical requirements. In the 19th century Darwin revolutionised this way of thinking, replacing the unity that comes from type with a unity that comes from historical continuity.

Goodwin's third example is the development of eyes. Eyes appear to be complex structures – so complex that they can seem to challenge the whole idea of non-teleological evolution. But despite this, eyes have evolved independently in at least 40 different lineages. The development of the eye is made possible by the fact that animal tissue, unlike plant tissue, can fold and buckle. This is possible because animal cells lack rigid walls and can therefore migrate over surfaces. Goodwin suggests that given the structural possibilities of animal tissue and the potential for morphological transformation, the repeated evolution of eyes isn't too surprising.

So we have two different accounts for the continuity of living organisms. One of these is grounded in historical continuity and argues that evolution is path-dependent, and the other argues that there are a limited number of patterns that development can follow. Fundamentally, this difference is an argument about where the constraints are located. In Maynard Smith's model, the more restrictive constraints are the constraints of molecular biology. In Goodwin's account, the constraints of physics are typically tighter than the constraints of molecular biology.

It is important to emphasise, however, that the protagonists themselves would not necessarily have looked at it this way. Maynard Smith writes that he has become more 'reductionist' over his career, his use of the term corresponding to 'reductivist' as I have been using it in this discussion. The success of molecular biology means that the interpretation of living organisms as pieces of molecular machinery has become more compelling. The gist of Goodwin's argument is that organisms are both functional and structural wholes. Unlike a mechanical object such as a clock, which has a functional unity, a living organism has both functional and structural unity. Whereas the parts of a clock are fabricated separately and then assembled, and can therefore also be dis-assembled, the parts of a living organism are transformations of regions of the whole as a consequence of the development of the system as a self-sustaining entity. In his book, Goodwin proposes replacing what he calls the science of quantities, the science of mechanical assembly, with a science of qualities, one that would focus on the expression of organic differentiation in integrated wholes.

Reading these books in conjunction with Schrödinger's essays suggests, somewhat ironically, that the reductivist biologist Maynard Smith is emphasising the discontinuity with physics, while the anti-reductivist biologist Goodwin is emphasising the continuity with physics. This makes sense if reductivism is at bottom the articulation of a method rather than a metaphysics. If it were metaphysics, the primitive components of biology would be the composite components of chemistry, and the primitive components of chemistry would be the composite components of physics. There would be only one science, and disciplinary boundaries would be fluid. If it is a method, a way of structuring explanations, the primitive components of biology don't have to be the composite components of chemistry.

There are a number of corollaries that follow from these different perspectives. The implication of Maynard Smith's argument is that the evolution of living organisms is path-dependent. Once the original plans were laid down, it was difficult for evolution to shift to another path because of the way the cascade of differentiation functions. The implication of this seems to be that if the initial body plans had been different, life on earth might have evolved quite differently. The implication of Goodwin's argument, on the other hand, is that the evolution of life on earth is not fundamentally path-dependent but was always going to look much as it does because of the constant repetition of forms due to the constraints of the underlying physics.

This difference of emphasis also draws attention to the fact that there are two different questions being asked by evolutionary biologists. Populations come from populations, and the first question is: how does a population with one distribution of characteristics and traits becomes a subsequent population with a different distribution of characteristics and traits? The second question is: why do we observe this set of characteristics and traits in living organisms on earth and not another set.

Characteristics and traits themselves come and go; they don't evolve in the way that populations of organisms evolve. In Maynard Smith's account molecular biology accounts for the continuity of characteristics and traits, and the changes in their distribution in the population of living organisms through time. However, it leaves the answer to the question as to why we observe this particular global set of characteristics and traits open. Why does life on earth take the form it does, and not some other form? This is the biologists' equivalent to the physicists' question: why is the universe the way it is and not some other way? Why is it this story and not some other story? Goodwin's book is an example of what an answer to that question might look like.

## Constraints-oriented explanations

Schrödinger wrote a second essay with the title called *Mind and Matter*, which was published just before his death in 1958. The topic is the physics and chemistry of the mind. What kind of material process is directly associated with consciousness? How can a collection of molecules originate introspective and intelligent minds? Schrödinger finds it impossible to form any idea about how this might occur. A lifetime later we are really no further forward. It isn't just a matter of understanding how minds are instantiated, but even being able to conceptualise the idea of an observer. What does it mean to be a spectator in the universe?

Schrödinger suggests that this problem takes a specific form for science, because scientific method is based on two general principles. The first is the principle of objectification, or what might be called the hypothesis of the real world. The hypothesis of the real world is another way of conceptualising materialism, the contrary of idealism. This creates a problem for science because the corollary of the principle of objectification is the exclusion of the subject of cognizance from the domain of science:

> *By this I mean the thing that is also frequently called the 'hypothesis of the real world' around us. I maintain that it amounts to a certain simplification which we adopt in order to master the infinitely intricate problem of nature. Without being aware of it and without being rigorously systematic about it, we exclude the Subject of Cognizance from the domain of nature that we endeavour to understand. We step*

> with our own person back into the part of an onlooker who does not belong to the world, which by this very procedure becomes an objective world.

This withdrawal is the scientist's opening gambit. However, the tactic cannot be sustained, because we must include our own and other people's bodies in the natural world, and we must assume that other people are also the seat of consciousness.

> Since there is no distinction between myself and others, but on the contrary full symmetry for all intents and purposes, I conclude that I myself form part of this real material world around me.

As a consequence, we must assume that we ourselves are part of the natural world both as a participant and as an observer. Having thus, as an opening gambit, excluded ourselves, in the middle game we now have to find a way of putting ourselves back into nature, an achievement that has proven to be elusive.

The second general principle is the idea of the understandability of nature. Schrödinger doesn't elaborate much on the principle of the understandability of nature in this essay, but does suggest that the development of quantum physics and the recognition of the uncertainty principle represents a partial abandonment of the idea. The uncertainty principle is the idea that, at the micro-scale, there is a limit to the precision with which both of some pairs of related physical properties can be known simultaneously. It is not therefore possible to determine precisely the state of a system at this scale. Whether this really is an epistemological barrier, or a reflection of the limitations of our current models of waves and particles, is an open question.

My view is that these principles create problems for scientific materialism, or what I have been calling 'materialist reductivism', rather than for modern science as such. To understand why, we need to dis-assemble the concept further. This is not straightforward. Scientific materialism is a paradigm. Paradigms are the organising principles of cognition and therefore difficult to subject to critical scrutiny. However, it's possible to dig out the main components. There are three: the causal closure of physics, determinism, and explanatory completeness. The causal closure of physics is the idea that the course of events is determined at the most micro-scale in a system; determinism is the idea that the evolution of every system follows a pattern of succession that is either invariable or probabilistic; and explanatory completeness is the idea that it is possible to build a comprehensive single-layered unequivocal explanation of how everything works.

The first component of the model is the assumption that events are determined at the smallest scale. Jerry Fodor, a sceptical reductivist, put it this way:

> *The idea that the basic laws are the laws about the smallest things has been central to the 'scientific world-view' ever since there started to be one. On the other hand, as far as I can see, it's not any sort of a priori truth. I suppose one can imagine a world where all the big things are made out of small things,*

> *and there are laws about the small things and there are laws about the big things, but some laws of the second kind don't derive from any laws of the first kind.*

A pragmatic and informal version of this idea is the one put forward by Stephen Hawking: a good scientific theory describes a large class of observations on the basis of a model that contains only a few arbitrary elements. In order to understand the significance of this we need to understand the layered structure of the model.

Metaphysically, modern science is a version of monism, which is the idea that there is an underlying unity behind the apparent diversity of events. In the case of modern science this is a question of scale. If you decompose everything to the smallest possible scale you will find a single set of components whose interactions can be described using a single set of principles. Since the unity of the model is at the level described by physics and chemistry, and the diversity is at the level described by the special sciences, it is therefore likely that the theories that best meet the criterion of a good scientific theory will be theories in physics and chemistry.

These layers are virtual layers. They are different ways of describing the same thing at different scales. The description at each scale is a complete description of the world. At the most fine-grained scale, the description is in terms of the models of quantum physics. At a lumpier scale the description is in terms of the chemical elements and molecules, thermodynamics and general relativity. Living systems can be described at a variety of scales: as populations of molecules, as populations of cells, as populations of organisms and as populations of species. An analysis in terms of molecular biology is as much a description of the whole of the biosphere as are descriptions in terms of cells or living organisms or species.

Because each layer is a complete description of the world, these layers are not shearing layers and the model is not one of parts and wholes. It is only when a macro-scale layer is partitioned into discrete wholes that micro-scale components can become parts of anything. When partitioned in this way into wholes and parts, it becomes clear that the component parts can continue to exist independently of the whole. For example, cells are temporary configurations of molecules. A cell is constructed from molecules, but the molecules exist independently of the cell; they come together transiently in the cell, then disperse. A cell cannot exist independently from a collection of molecules, but it can exist independently of any given set of molecules. The same relationship holds between cells and organisms as between organisms and populations, and indeed between anything that can be analysed into parts and wholes.

The causal closure of physics is the idea that every event is determined at the micro-scale of particle physics. The argument is that there is a complete description of how micro-scale components behave entirely in terms of micro-scale interactions and, since the description at each scale is a complete description of the world, there cannot therefore be any determination of events at any other scale. The idea that the determination of events happens at the smallest scale implies the causal completeness of physics, because physics contains the description of the microscale in the scientific picture. I suspect that something like this lies behind the philosophical commitment, reported by Corey Powell, to the idea that general relativity will turn out to be an aspect of quantum theory.

It is the casual closure of physics in combination with monism that creates reductivism. The idea of the causal completeness of physics should be distinguished from the idea of the causal completeness of the physical. The difference is that causal completeness within a monist framework implies reductivism, whereas causal completeness in a dualist framework implies only that the physical world is completely described but leaves open the possibility that there are other domains. This would mean that physics isn't a description of everything. This is a Roman Catholic position, for example.

The second component of the model is the determinist assumption that systems evolve in a pattern of succession of cause and effect. The pattern-of-succession model of change was developed in the 18th century as a response to the scientific revolution of the 17th century and started to take the place of the Aristotelian model of change in the same way that modern science started to take the place of Aristotelian science.

Traditionally, causes answered the question: why do things become what they are? Aristotle called them *aiton*: the explanation for how and why things come about, from which the term 'aetiology' derives. He identified four causes or explanations: the material explanation, the formal explanation, the functional explanation and the efficient explanation. Material, formal and functional explanations are clear. The efficient explanation is the agency that brings everything together. This is a model of responsibility based on the image of the artisan and the artefact. Something is what it is because some agent shaped some material in order to carry out some function. The philosophical term is *hylomorphism*, from the Greek words for *wood* and *shaping*.

The Aristotelian model of the four causes was much baggier than the pattern-of-succession model. There were two basic aspects to the model. The first is that there is in everything an inherent movement towards actualisation, something Aristotle called *entelechia,* a term that captures the idea that everything has a *telos*, an end point or destination towards which it is evolving. In the Aristotelian version the origin of the movement towards actualisation is in some way inherent in the world rather than being outside it, as Plato had argued; the motivating dynamic is immanent rather than transcendent.

The second aspect of the multiplicity of causes is that each operates as a constraint on the others. Although this is traditionally called the doctrine of the four causes, it could also be called the doctrine of the four constraints. For the agent, the materials available constrain the form, and the form constrains the choice of materials. Similarly, the function constrains the form and the materials, and the materials and the form constrain the function.

As a consequence, an explanation has two aspects. There is a description of the forces that are driving change in the system, providing the motivation and dynamic, and there is a description of the constraints under which the system is evolving. Everything human and everything natural has a *telos*, which is the source of change in the system, but the multiplicity and diversity of the world means that these operate as mutual constraints.

This was the default model of change in Western thinking before the development of modern science, and can be applied to both the human and the natural order. However, as a consequence of the development of modern science, the explanations of the natural order and the human order came apart. This led to the development of the idea of the evolution of a natural system as a sequence of events explained as a pattern of succession. The earlier state of the system determines the later state of the system. Compared with the traditional teleological model, the pattern-of-succession model sees the evolution of a system as a journey away from an origination point rather than a journey towards a destination.

The elaboration of the idea of explanation as pattern of succession is associated with David Hume, who developed the idea in his *Essay Concerning Human Understanding*, published in 1748. This is how it is described by Christopher Hitchcock in the *Stanford Encyclopedia of Philosophy*:

> *According to David Hume, causes are invariably followed by their effects: 'We may define a cause to be an object, followed*

> by another, and where all the objects similar to the first, are followed by objects similar to the second'. ... Attempts to analyse causation in terms of invariable patterns of succession are referred to as 'regularity theories' of causation. There are a number of well-known difficulties with regularity theories, and these may be used to motivate probabilistic approaches to causation.

In its original form the idea was that systems evolved in an invariable pattern of succession, because an invariable pattern of succession maps intuitively to the mechanical picture of the world. But the development of quantum theories has led to the recognition of probabilistic patterns of succession. Invariable patterns of succession map to classical mechanics and probabilistic patterns of succession map to quantum mechanics.

The third component of the model is the idea that it is plausible to aspire to the goal of a complete, objective and unequivocal understanding of how everything works. This is what Schrödinger means by the assumption of the understandability of nature. In the 17$^{th}$ and 18$^{th}$ centuries this idea was encapsulated in the principle of sufficient reason. The modern version of the principle is attributed to Leibniz, writing some forty years before Hume. The principle of sufficient reason is the idea that there must always be a sufficient explanation for why some event occurred and not some other event. Every effect must have at least one sufficient cause, and every cause must lead to only one effect. It should always be possible to explain a subsequent state by pointing to the antecedent state.

How does the principle of sufficient reason relate to the scientific method? Why must it be the working assumption? Another way of conceptualising the principle of sufficient reason is that the relationship between the earlier state and the later state in the evolution of a system can be one-to-one or many-to-one, but never one-to-many. A system in which the relationship between earlier and later states is one-to-many will pose a problem for science because it will be difficult in such a situation to meet Stephen Hawking's second criterion for a good scientific theory, which is that *it must make definite predictions about the results of future observations.* Scientific method is likely to interpret the observation of a one-to-many relationship in the evolution of a system as a problem with the theory being tested, or a failure in the design of the experiment, rather than a discovery about the system.

In modern thinking the understandability of nature is more likely to be made in terms of an appeal to the idea that there are laws of nature. This argues that we are able to understand natural systems because the way they evolve is determined by regular principles, natural laws, which we can discover and describe. These are the rules of the game. Every event can be accounted for by showing how the sequence of events is an instantiation of these principles. However, by itself the idea that there are natural laws would mean little more than that where we find regularities in the way natural systems evolve, there are regularities in the way natural systems evolve. The idea that natural laws are in some way determining the evolution of a system implicitly requires something like the principle of sufficient reason to provide the heft.

The principle of the understandability of nature is independent of the hypothesis of the real world. In fact, there is an obvious sense in which the understandability of nature and the hypothesis of the real world are in conflict. The idealist argues that we can assume that the world has been constructed to be understood. The hypotheses of the real world, on the other hand, says that nature is independent of the way we think. It says that the way the world is is independent of the way the mind works, and nature doesn't depend on there being a spectator to observe or to conceptualise it.

It may still be true that the world was constructed to be understood, but we would have to work this out from observation. What order does nature have to have, and why would it have more order than is necessary? We could discover that the world evolves according to the principle of sufficient reason, but we shouldn't assume it. In fact, we should assume the contrary in order to be confident that, were we ever to come to that conclusion, it really was a discovery.

However, in order to make progress, science tends to assume the understandability of nature, if only as a working principle. At the same time, because of the hypothesis of the real world, the scientist must assume that this is an accidental rather than a necessary feature of the world. However, if it is an accidental feature, then there is no real basis for the idea that a complete and unequivocal understanding of nature is possible. This, I think, is the reason scientific materialism in the end doesn't actually escape from the idealist framework; it is at bottom another form of metaphysical speculation that assumes the cosmos is constructed in an inherently understandable manner.

These three ideas – causal closure at the micro-scale, the pattern-of-succession approach to explanation, and the assumption of the understandability of nature – are the three load-bearing assumptions behind the reductive and determinist interpretation of science.

How persuasive is this model? There are a number of problems. With regard to causal closure at the micro-scale, four objections suggest themselves. Firstly, it is not intuitively obvious why the micro-scale should be privileged in this way, since scientific models work at all scales. And if there can be one set of organising principles, why can there not be more than one? What sort of constraint is operating?

Secondly, if everything is determined at the smallest scale, then why does the observable world at the macro-scale exhibit the order and reliability that it does? The challenge for any version of monism is to explain why at the same time everything is the same and everything is different. If the determination of events is entirely within the level of unity, how do you explain the diversity? How do large-scale structures persist and evolve? It cannot be a causal interaction, because the layers are not separate events but alternative descriptions of the same event. There is no gap between them in which an interaction of any kind could operate. If everything is determined at the micro-scale, then modern science itself is just the interactions of physics aggregated and viewed from a sufficient distance. The scientific community is the micro-scale world of particle physics reflecting on itself. This is an explanatory chasm no-one, as far as I know, has ever had any success at all in bridging.

Thirdly, it means that human agency is impossible, because everything is already fully determined at the micro-scale of quantum physics. In this model, if mental events are explained in terms of meaning, value and purpose, there are too many causes. Monism implies that mental events are physical events. But mental events are experienced as teleological, as a journey to a destination, whereas physical events can only be a journey from a point of origin. If events at the micro-scale determine events at the macro-scale then our experience of human agency is either an illusion or the manifestation of an as yet unknown parallel mechanism at the micro-scale of physics. This is a substantial loss of explanatory scope without any compensating gain. We are giving something up – the ability to give macro-scale explanations for macro-scale phenomenon – and getting nothing in return because, at least for now, there is no such explanation of human agency or experience in physics.

Fourthly, I am not convinced that the scientific model that we have matches the requirements of scientific materialism. We don't need to climb the stack from quantum mechanics to the human mind to observe the diversity of scientific explanations and the differences between deterministic and probabilistic mechanics, between statistical and mechanical order, between self-organising and self-sustaining systems and between mechanical assembly and organic differentiation as processes of development. This diversity is mirrored in our experience of the way modern science is developing. Instead of the sciences converging in a unified science, as you might expect if there were an underlying unity, recent experience has been of a proliferation and diversification of autonomous special sciences.

What might an alternative picture look like? It is in the context of scale that we can understand the significance of the possibilities of stability and complexity. Why do human beings have to be so much larger than the molecules of which they are composed? It is because sufficient stability is only realised at the molecular scale and the complexity of life and intelligence is only possible on a platform constructed from complex molecules.

It's in the context of scale that the importance of symmetry to the scientific picture can be understood. Symmetry is the idea that a system can remain unchanged in some aspect through a transformation such as rotation or transposition in time or space. The fundamental principles of science are principles of conservation, and for every principle of conservation there is a related symmetry.

The scientific method assumes symmetry through time. The repetition of events that is the consequence of the symmetry of the micro-scale through time is the basis of the scientific method. If you can't repeat an experiment at a later time, you can't get a scientific result. But there is no symmetry across scale. In the micro-scale worlds in which scientific knowledge is tested, there is symmetry through time. In the macro-scale worlds of cosmology, the evolution of life and the acquisition of culture, there is no symmetry through time: everything has a memory, and therefore everything has a history.

If there is no symmetry across scale then there is no difficulty imagining symmetry through time at one scale and the absence of symmetry through time at another scale. Furthermore, if the micro-scale is constant and the macro-scale is evolving, it is much more plausible to suppose that the evolution of the cosmos is being driven at the macro-scale and that the constant micro-scale is functioning as a constraint on what histories are possible at the macro-scale.

The objection to the reductivist assumption of causal closure therefore is that it is unnecessary and pre-emptively limiting. A similar objection applies to the determinist assumption that systems evolve in an invariable or probabilistic pattern of succession. The model of explanation as a pattern of cause and effect not only fails to describe the way that scientific explanations now function, but also provides little traction in understanding human experience.

This is not a new idea; it was already being suggested by Bertrand Russell in 1913. In his article on the metaphysics of causation in the *Stanford Encyclopedia of Philosophy*, Jonathan Schaffer quotes Russell's *On the Notion of Cause*:

> *The law of causality, I believe, like much that passes muster among philosophers, is a relic of a bygone age, surviving, like the monarchy, only because it is erroneously supposed to do no harm.*

Partly, this is a reflection of the way the sciences have developed. Often, a pattern of succession of events was discovered before the underlying explanatory model. For example, Mendel's experiments with pea plants showed the patterns of inheritance long before the underlying genetic mechanism that explained it was understood. Similarly, the construction of the periodic table of the elements pre-dates the underlying explanatory model in terms of particle physics. Science at the end of the 20th century looked very different from science at the end of the 19th.

If this is the case, why hasn't causation simply been eliminated? Schaffer goes on to explain:

> *The main objection…is that causation is too central to eliminate. Causation, according to various contemporary philosophers, is required for the analysis of metaphysical concepts such as persistence, scientific concepts such as explanation and disposition, epistemic concepts such as perception and warrant, ethical concepts such as action and responsibility, mental concepts such as functional role and conceptual content, and linguistic concepts such as reference. Elimination is not just unjustified; it would be catastrophic.*

He also makes a suggestion regarding a path forward, which is to retain the approach to explanation, recognising causality as a possible conceptual model of explanation, without supposing that cause and effect are in any way fundamental constituents out there in the real world.

> *This middle position would claim to explain both the failures of conceptual analyses, and the disappearance of causation from fundamental physics.*

Today, an explanation is achieved through the successful application of a model. Is the target system within the domain of application of a particular model? If quantified models can be applied to a system, then predictions can be made about what the quantifiable state of the system will be at some future time and the path along which it will evolve. If the predictions reliably match the observed outcome, the system can be taken to be within the domain of application of the model. The same methodology can be used to work backwards from the state of the system as it is observed to what it must have been at some point in time in the past. The limiting case is the moment of origin, the big bang, conceived as a singularity where the models no longer apply.

These kinds of arguments lead to a puzzle. Why do we persist it making unnecessary assumptions that only make the world we observe and inhabit problematic? Why is the way that we think about explanation different from the way we actually explain events? Schaffer suggests a kind of sunk cost argument, but I think the deeper answer is that, as Schrödinger argued, scientific materialism is at bottom the expression of an aspiration to understand, and for understanding to be achieved we must assume everything is understandable. The components of this model are independent of each other, but as a package it is the understandability of nature that holds everything together and provides the motivation.

There is a logic to this. The enterprise to gain a complete understanding of nature is most likely to be feasible if we can assume a reductive and deterministic framework. Reduction through analysis is a closed process that it might be possible to complete, whereas synthesis through systems thinking is inevitably open-ended. Similarly, it might be possible to fully understand a system that is evolving in an invariable or probabilistic pattern of succession in a way that isn't possible with regard to a constrained, open-ended system.

What seems to have happened is this. In the course of the scientific revolution of the 17th century, the idea that there was an inherent teleology in the way systems evolve was discarded as unnecessary. Explanations no longer appeared to require assumptions about purpose or destination. What could be discerned was a reliable pattern of succession of events of cause and effect. But this was an observation, not an explanation.

An explanation requires a description both of what drives the evolution of a system and what constrains it. It is this requirement of explanation that leads, as an alternative to teleology, to appeals to the principle of sufficient reason and the idea that systems evolve according to laws of nature. They provide the mixture of something to push or pull and something to constrain, that explanation requires.

Another solution to this problem would be some form of dualism, which would partition the world into natural systems and non-natural systems, such that the reductive and deterministic model only applies to natural systems. However, this introduces some obvious problems of explaining how natural systems and non-natural systems are supposed to interact and is, in my view, unnecessary. A better solution is to retain the monism and the hypothesis of the real world as the two minimal assumptions, but drop the other structural assumptions in the model: the determination of events at the micro-scale, the pattern-of-succession model of explanation, and the aspiration for a single-layered, comprehensive and unequivocal explanation of nature.

In order to do this, we need to adopt what I call a constraints-oriented approach to explanation. An explanation should still have two components, one necessary, the other optional. The necessary component is a description of the constraints under which the system is evolving. The optional component is a description of the forces, if there are any, which drive the evolution of a system. The actual path the evolution of the system takes must fall within the constraints. The constraints define the boundaries of the possible; and the motivating forces, if there are any, explain the actual path taken within those boundaries. While there may be no foreground dynamic, there is always a set of background constraints. This requires a change in focus from the foreground to the background. Instead of asking how the system functions if we hold the background steady, we should be asking how systems of this kind subject to this set of constraints would evolve.

What are the advantages of constraints-oriented thinking? Firstly, it aligns with modern methodology and the application of scientific models. The methodology of modern science and the models of modern physics are constraints-oriented ways of thinking. Facts, such as the universal attraction that is gravity, are constraints. Both quantum mechanics and classical mechanics are grounded in a set of fundamental constraints expressed as principles of conservation (of energy, of momentum, of charge) – principles that are themselves connected to the symmetries in the universe. As Feynman puts it:

> *a fact that most physicists still find somewhat staggering, a most profound and beautiful thing, is that, in quantum mechanics, for each of the rules of symmetry there is a corresponding conservation law; there is a definite connection between the laws of conservation and the symmetries of physical laws.*

Secondly, it supports the explanation of multi-layered structures with a variety of drivers. Only the micro-scale is persistent. Larger scale structures come and go. But if the larger scale structures are constraints that are important for how a system behaves at the micro-scale, then an explanation of events at the micro-scale is never going to be sufficient. This doesn't mean that you cannot predict how a system will evolve at the micro-scale, but it does mean that the scope of the explanation is constrained. It won't necessarily tell you why the system is the way that it is, only that within a specified set of constraints we may expect it to behave in a predictable fashion. In this model, systems at different scales function as mutual constraints.

The third advantage follows from this. The same model is applicable both to the natural order and the human order. As things stand, there is an obvious gap between the scientific description of natural systems and significant aspects of familiar experience. We have neither a holistic understanding that reaches from particle physics to moral accountability and the creative arts, nor an account of why they are discontinuous and incommensurable.

Constraints-oriented explanations are both simpler and more comprehensive. For example, in modern industrial societies, we live very different lives from our ancestors, we have different pressures and different opportunities. Why is that? It's possible we are different people, and you could construct an account that started from this premise and tried to understand those differences and show how they account for the differences in the way we live. Or you could start from the simpler proposition that we are much the same people; our biological systems, our emotional structures and our cognitive capabilities haven't really changed. What is different is the context in which those drivers operate, so that modern populations live under a fundamentally different set of constraints, not just of geography and climate and population, but also of cultural acquisition, science, technology and social organisation.

Fourthly, a constraints-oriented model of explanation doesn't impose an interpretation on events; the method doesn't determine the object. The weakness of the reductive and deterministic model of explanation is that the assumptions mean that only one kind of system and only one kind of explanation is possible. The advantage of a constraints-oriented model of explanation is that it supports every kind of system and all kinds of explanation: deterministic, non-deterministic, random, and reasoned. A single-layered explanation is a special case of a multi-layered explanation. But if only a single-layered explanation is acceptable, multi-layered explanations become impossible.

Schrödinger's own conclusion is the most plausible one. If the functioning of the micro-scale of physics follows regularities that we describe as the laws of nature, and at the same time we experience ourselves as intelligent beings who see into the future and make decisions, then the only conclusion can be that, just as the micro-scale of physics constrains the macro-scale of human experience, our decision-making at the macro-scale of human experience is constraining the behaviour of the systems at the micro-scale of physics.

The disadvantage of constraints-oriented thinking, from the perspective of the understandability of nature, is that constraints-oriented approaches to explanation do not give the same level of completeness and finality. Constraints-oriented systems must be accompanied by constrained explanations rather than unequivocal and universal explanations. A constraints-oriented model is non-deterministic and therefore places a limitation on the possibility of understanding. If we accept the possibility of constrained explanation and multi-layered models of reality, of systems of systems partitioned by shearing layers, it is likely that at some level the world will always remain inscrutable and the goal of a complete understanding of nature will not be realisable.

# Science and secularism

Is there a genuine conflict between science and religion? Are they contesting some of the same ground or are they, as Stephen Jay Gould somewhat grandly proposed, 'non-overlapping magisteria'? Perhaps, more fundamentally, isn't the real conflict between secularism and religion, with science finding itself being pressed into service as an auxiliary? There are, as always, three battlefields: metaphysics, ethics and epistemology.

The conflict between religion and secularism is a question of metaphysics. In the west when we think about religious thinking, we tend to assume it is in the form of theism, and as a consequence we tend to think about religion as something primarily requiring belief, instead of something primarily requiring practice. But doubt is as much a part of the religious sensibility as belief, and theism is only one kind of religion – importantly, a kind that creates difficulties that aren't applicable to religious thinking more broadly. Buddhism has no creator god, but it is not secular. Recognising this, I think it would bring a helpful clarity to disentangle belief from religion. Belief is a question for epistemology: what can we know? Religion is a question for metaphysics: what can we hope for?

What is common to all religions and distinguishes religious thinking from secular thinking is that it assumes that at some level there is a moral continuity between the human and the natural. In the west this unity is understood as the operation of providence. Karma is perhaps the equivalent in the east. What lies at the core of secular thinking, on the other hand, is the sense that nature is neutral, indifferent to the fate of humanity.

The secular and the religious are sensibilities more than they are conclusions from observation or discoveries. In his review of the scientist and theologian John Polkinghorne's book about the end of the world, Freeman Dyson writes:

> *At the end of his two scientific chapters, Polkinghorne summarizes their findings in a single sentence: 'From its own unaided resources, natural science can do no more than present us with the contrast of a finely tuned and fruitful universe which is condemned to ultimate futility'.*

This is the religious sensibility looking for convergence between the human and the natural and, failing to find it, concluding that everything is pointless. A secular sensibility, on the other hand would not be seeking purpose, value and meaning here. Rather than finding futility in these absences, it would see challenges and possibilities: a reliable and stable platform, often intricate, sometimes sublime; a background, not a foreground.

This metaphysical difference has an ethical and practical significance. Are human destiny and natural destiny woven into a single cosmos, or is nature a neutral stage, a terrain for exploration and adventure? These paths lead to different kinds of belief and practice, and different kinds of institution. Can we express this conflict succinctly given that beliefs, practices and institutions differ so considerably? My suggestion is that what is common can be found in the idea that while secular thinking casts humanity in a principal role in the performance, religious thinking offers it only a supporting role – an indispensable one, but a supporting one nonetheless.

John Gray, in his provocative polemic *Straw Dogs*, defines modern humanism as a belief in the inevitability of progress and the specialness of humanity. This specialness implies that unlike every other animal, humanity can, through the pursuit of scientific knowledge and technological invention, become master of its own destiny. Gray sees the specialness accorded to humanity in modern humanism as a continuation of the specialness accorded it in Christian theology. However, I think this misses the significant elevation in status that accompanies the change.

The force of this distinction only really became apparent to me while reading Sartre's lecture *Existentialism Is a Humanism* and Heidegger's response *The Letter on Humanism*. The exchange is concerned with the ethical implications of existentialism, and there is a clear contrast between Sartre's ethics of action, decision and responsibility, and the ethics of dwelling, listening and safeguarding that we find in Heidegger.

For Sartre, we are condemned to be free; we must improvise creatively because there is no script and no program, no sign in the heavens to discern, no path to follow. To be condemned to be free is to be condemned to the role of protagonist, and bad faith is the attempt to shirk that responsibility. Sartre took his inspiration from Heidegger, but whereas Sartre was an urban philosopher and an atheist, Heidegger was an agrarian philosopher with a religious sensibility, and he didn't accept Sartre's interpretation of his ideas.

In Heidegger's view, although humanity has an indispensable role, it is a secondary role. In the *Letter on Humanism* he writes that *'Der Mensch ist nicht der Herr des Seienden. Der Mensch ist der Hirt des Seins'*, usually translated as *'Man is not the lord of beings. Man is the shepherd of Being'*. Unfortunately, this translation obscures the meaning. I would gloss the statement to mean that humanity is not the master of the observable world (*das Seiende*), but rather a servant of the process (*das Sein*) through which it becomes observable. For Heidegger, humanity's destiny has already been determined; the question is whether we can understand the casting and accept the role.

George Steiner suggested an affinity between Heidegger and the poet Gerard Manley Hopkins. Although Hopkins was a Jesuit priest, he was inspired more by John Duns Scotus than the Jesuit's official theologian Thomas Aquinas. Heidegger was also briefly a Jesuit novice, and his *habilitation* thesis was on Duns Scotus categories. Hopkins invented the term *'inscape'* to mean the pattern of attributes that composes the individuality of a thing, and *'instress'* to mean the force that binds these attributes together and, as it were, projects them into the mind of an observer. What underlies this way of thinking is the ancient idea that the reality of the world is something that can only be received, not something that can be actively discovered; that the movement to understanding originates in the object, not in the subject; and that therefore only when action and thought have been stilled can this reality be apprehended.

Because religion and secularism are metaphysical positions, it should be possible to resolve the argument, at least to the point of deciding where the weight of evidence lies. What kind of evidence might be presented? Science is consistent with secularism; secularism doesn't expect to find meaning, purpose and value in nature, and science doesn't find them there. But if some version of the religious understanding turns out to be the true picture, would we expect to be able to detect this using the scientific method? I think the answer is no. Freeman Dyson's mystical reductivism is a reflection of his scepticism about how much we actually know. Scientific materialism, on the other hand, is a reflection of scientific and technological confidence and optimism; it is the kind of metaphysics you get if you make confident judgements about how much has already been achieved and how much can and will be achieved in the future.

It is this cognitive optimism and confidence that Gray identifies as the basis for modern humanism, and it is this kind of optimism and confidence he wants to undermine in order to create an opening to an alternative model of how to live. But his solution, which is for us to become simple participants in nature in the way that animals are, seems to me to be unworkable – even if it were desirable: we can't stop being introspective beings; we are, as Sartre suggested, condemned to freedom.

That being said, I am sympathetic to Gray's argument. I hesitate to consider myself a humanist. We only qualify to sit at this table contingently because we are intelligent beings. Should we ever come into contact with a non-terrestrial civilisation, one on the same level as our own, we will meet not on the basis of a common humanity but on the basis of a common intelligence. Furthermore, to approach the world only through one's own predicament ensures that it is never possible to escape that contingency. If we are to live on this planet, we must learn to accommodate and adapt ourselves to it, and not try to shape it around ourselves, as humanism does.

There is no need for religion in the scientific model and nothing in the familiar observable world, at the scale at which we live, makes more sense or becomes more meaningful through making religious assumptions; if anything, such assumptions make the world more problematic. This is the real disagreement between secularism and religion. The natural world doesn't have to supply meaning, purpose and value; there is no deficit that requires a remedy; and there is no need to go looking beyond the natural to a providential order. A secular sensibility is quite comfortable with the idea that the cosmos is inscrutable, undetermined and open-ended, and life ultimately an improvisation.

CHAPTER FOUR

# AUTHENTIC INTELLIGENCE

## The imitation game

In a paper published in 1950, Alan Turing considered the question whether or not an algorithmic machine could think. He suggested that because thinking is difficult to conceptualise, it would make more sense to ask a slightly different question, namely: is it possible to imagine a machine that could pass for a human being? The test would be success at playing 'the imitation game', a parlour game in which contestants try to pass for someone else.

Turing argued that a machine could successfully pass this test. He considers a number of possible objections, but they are all really variations on one basic idea. This can be expressed in two ways: as the argument that being human requires attributes such as a soul or consciousness that computers don't have; or as the argument that some tasks that human beings can accomplish, such as those involving creativity and innovation, are impossible for a computer to complete.

Turing subscribed to a version of scientific and technological optimism. His response to these objections was that while many problems couldn't be solved with the technology of his day, they would be solvable with some future technology, and the fact that we don't understand the rules governing some activity now doesn't necessarily imply that there are no rules to discover. We cannot know the limits of machine capability, and therefore we will never be in a position to say that some task can never be accomplished. The argument became an unresolvable dispute between two *nevers*: the never in the argument that machines will never match human capabilities; and the never in the argument that we will never be in a position to come to that conclusion.

However, the idea of the imitation game can be taken in another direction, more intrepid and therefore more interesting. If machines can successfully imitate intelligent beings without being themselves intelligent beings, then perhaps human beings are also successfully imitating intelligent beings without actually being intelligent beings.

Why might this be an interesting idea? The problem it addresses is this. We successfully complete calculations such as $12 \div 3 = 4$ all the time, and the correctness of the calculation is a function of its meaning. But, according to the materialist reductivist interpretation of modern science, meaning is not present at the micro-scale at which the evolution of events is determined. If the evolution of the world is a function of events determined at the micro-scale, and only these events, then it follows that authentic intelligence at the macro-scale isn't possible. But, if this is right, how can the macro-scale performance, the successful completion of the calculation, be so reliably achieved?

What applies to meaning applies equally to value and purpose. None of these are concepts in modern science. So more generally, given the hypothesis of materialist reductivism, how do we explain the reliability, order and resilience of the world of meanings, values and purposes that we inhabit?

The imitation game could be a solution. Just as computers track the evolution of a calculation without being directly aware of its meaning, so perhaps human beings also track the evolution of the calculation without being directly aware of any meaning. And perhaps, in a similar way, human beings are able to track the evolution of a course of action governed by values and purposes without being directly aware of those values and purposes.

Materialist reduction isn't the only possible approach to the interpretation of this situation, and therefore the imitation game isn't the only potential solution. Two alternative interpretations are what I have been calling idealist and mystical reductivism. In both cases the idea is that meaning, value and purpose do in fact inform the fabric and structure of the universe at all scales in a way that we cannot yet comprehend. If meaning is embedded in the system all the way down, then there is less of a puzzle. What we perceive as the reliable evolution of the system through the expression of meaning, value and purpose at the macro-scale is a reflection of the same meaning, value and purpose operating at the micro-scale. The difficulty with these solutions is that there is really no detail as to how they might work with the science that we have.

For this reason, the prevailing reductivist interpretation of modern science is scientific materialism and it is from this perspective that the idea of the imitation game suggests a possible solution to the problem. Computers can imitate intelligence without being conscious, let alone having a capacity for introspection. The idea behind the imitation game is that the human mind is an algorithm processor in a similar way to a computer. We are not able to apprehend directly the meaning of the calculation, but we can nevertheless successfully perform the calculation. Very much like a computer, a human being functions as an intelligent being without actually being one.

How does imitation work as a solution to the problem? The most significant feature of the functioning of a modern computer is that meaning drives process. The imitation game proposal starts from a different assumption, which is that process preserves meaning. This is often stated in grammatical terms, following John Haugeland's dictum that *if you take care of the syntax, the semantics will take care of itself.* Here is how Daniel Dennett puts it:

> *A genuine semantic engine, responding* directly *to meanings, is like a perpetual motion machine – physically impossible. So how can brains accomplish their appointed task? By being syntactic engines that* track *or* mimic *the competence of the impossible semantic engine.*

This brings us to the crux of the argument. A computer is such a syntactic engine. When it is programmed to carry out a calculation, the state changes in the computer track the semantics of the calculation through an analogy of form. But a computer has to be programmed by a software engineer who has grasped the meaning of the calculation. But what if the software engineer who writes the program is also only ever tracking meaning rather than actually responding to meaning directly? This would mean that the system as a whole, the engineer and the engine, only ever imitates the behaviour of the impossible authentically intelligent system.

How does the model work? The architecture is combinatorial and bottom-up. At the micro-scale are the simple instructions that make up the basic moves in the algorithm, and at the macro-scale the complex routines that operate at the familiar human scale. Simple primitive instructions are combined into more functional routines that can carry out more complex tasks. For convenience we usually try to explain events at a summary scale by adopting perspectives that Dennett calls 'stances'. We may, for example, adopt the intentional stance and tell the story as if there were intention in the system. However, these stances are epistemological rather than metaphysical: they are ways of knowing rather than ways of being. There is an assumption in this model that the instructions that make up the algorithms dovetail with the interactions of physics, chemistry and biology, but it's not clear how this is happening.

In place of computer programmers, biological evolution is nature's software engineer. Computers have been developed to imitate intelligent beings, and in, a similar fashion, human beings have evolved through natural selection to imitate intelligent beings. One difference in method is that while a software engineer works top down, taking a complex action and breaking it down into simpler and simpler routines until it can be captured as a set of very simple instructions that can be run as an algorithm, evolution works bottom up, starting with the simplest instructions and then assembling them into more and more functional components until they perform complex actions.

Why is a genuine semantic engine impossible? It is too easy to get diverted at this point into an argument about whether biological evolution, which has no forward-looking capability, could have generated organisms at a human level of complexity. But what baseline for time versus complexity is being used to suggest this isn't possible? A better question in this context is to ask why a population of authentic intelligent beings couldn't evolve. What constraint is operating? There are physical constraints on what is evolutionarily possible. There are path dependencies and process limitations. For example, unlike engineering, where failed experiments can be discarded, on an evolutionary path every generation must be viable, and therefore some modifications are not possible because there is a generation on the path that would not be viable. But these limitations don't obviously block the evolution of authentically intelligent beings.

The answer, I think, is that evolution is here only an auxiliary. Biological evolution is a macro-scale process. The constraint that is operating in this model is the assumption that events are wholly determined at the micro-scale. It isn't a question of what configurations of molecules are possible. The micro-scale events that support an imitation semantic engine would be the same as the micro-scale events that support a genuine semantic engine. The issue is at what scale the driving motivation is operating. What causes the adjustments and the accommodations in the system? An authentic intelligence can only happen at a macro-scale, the scale of relatively large living organisms, and not at the micro-scale of physics and chemistry. Therefore, the idea is that authentic intelligent beings cannot evolve, not because authentic intelligence is beyond the scope of evolution, but because authentic intelligence is not possible if every event is fully determined at the micro-scale.

What I am calling the imitation game is an attempt to describe the mind within the constraints of a reductivist and deterministic interpretation of science. How you interpret this probably depends on where you start from. If you share the underlying assumptions of scientific materialism, then something like this has to be made to work and the gaps and limitations must be interpreted as the inevitable features of a work in progress. If you don't share the underlying assumptions, then all this effort is trying to provide a solution to a problem that doesn't need to be solved, and the gaps and limitations look like confirmations that the original assumptions were flawed.

My view is that the idea of imitation intelligence and the complex infrastructure of tracking and illusion that scientific materialism requires is over-complicated and unnecessary. The simpler hypothesis is that the mind is metaphysically what it appears to be. The mind is a macro-scale event and the logic of the performance is a macro-scale logic. Human beings are capable of a direct response to meaning because we have a capacity for introspection, and from this flows the possibility of a sense of self and ethical accountability. This hypothesis is consistent with the idea that the mind has a physics and a chemistry, and also with the idea that the mind is the outcome of an evolutionary process. The apparent conflict is the consequence of a misleading metaphysics that has been imposed on the scientific picture of the world.

## The persistence of meaning

There are two different sets of questions that can be asked about authentic intelligence. The first set of questions is about consciousness, and these have proved largely intractable so far, even difficult to frame. How can there be observers in the world? We have the experience, but lack a conceptual model.

The second set of questions is about meaning. In this set there is, firstly, the question regarding the meaning of meaning: why *does* 12÷3 = 4? Secondly there is the question about how meaning can persist through the state changes in an underlying physical system. Each time we do the calculation 12÷3 = 4 we reliably get the correct answer and this correctness is a function of the meaning of the calculation. This second question is now easier to grapple with, because the modern digital computer demonstrates exactly how meaning can persist through the state changes in a physical system functioning as a base.

Meaning can persist in a digital computer system because an analogy of form has been created. The most significant components in an electronic computer are the transistors that function as switches. When passed through a transistor, a high voltage input is switched to a low voltage output and, conversely, a low voltage input to a high voltage output. The insight that underlies the modern digital computer is that if high voltage and low voltage are conceptualised as 1 and 0, then the model of an electronic switch has exactly the same form as the model of the logical operation of negation in a binary system, where the negation of one is zero and the negation of zero is one.

In a modern computer, transistors are organised into components called 'logic gates'. How a logic gate works depends on the number of transistors and whether they are linked together in parallel or in sequence. Engineers building relay systems for communications networks began experimenting early on with designs for logic gates, but rigour and standardisation were bought to the process through the systematic application of Boolean algebra. This project was brought to completion by Claude Shannon, one of the pioneers of information theory, in a paper published in 1938.

Boolean algebra is generated from combinations of three types of operation: conjunction, disjunction and negation. Negation is the simple flipping of one to zero or true to false, and therefore has one binary input and one binary output. In contrast, the operations of conjunction and disjunction operate on two binary inputs and generate a single binary output.

The logic gate that performs the conjunction operation is called an *and-gate* because it carries out the logical operation *p and q*. In an *and-gate* the transistors are organised in sequence. Conversely, the logic gate that performs the disjunction operation is called an *or-gate* because it carries out the logical operation *p or q*. In an *or-gate* the transistors are organised in parallel.

However, in Boolean algebra both algebraic operations and logical operations can be represented in terms of a single set of binary operations. In Boolean arithmetic there are only two operations, addition and multiplication. At this level, arithmetic and logic have the same form: the logical expression of conjunction *p and q* can also be the algebraic expression of multiplication *a x b* and the logical expression of disjunction *p or q* can also be the algebraic expression of addition *a + b*.

This commonality of form can be shown as follows. In Boolean arithmetic 1 x 1 = 1. If you multiply any of the other input combinations the answer will be zero: 1 x 0 = 0; 0 x 1 = 0 and 0 x 0 = 0. Similarly, the logical statement *p and q* is true only if both p and q are true, otherwise it is false. In logic the values 'true' and 'false' map to 1 and 0 respectively, so represented in binary form, if either p = 0 or q = 0, then the output will be 0; and if both inputs are 1 the output will also be 1.

The same commonality of form applies with regard to disjunction. If the inputs are 0 and 0, the output will be 0. If the inputs are 1 and 0, 0 and 1, or 1 and 1 the output will be 1. Thus, in Boolean arithmetic 1 + 0 = 1, 0 + 1 = 1 and 1 + 1 = 1 but 0 + 0 = 0. Similarly, *p or q* will be true if either *p* or *q* is true or both are true and false if both *p* and *q* are false. Arithmetic and logic thus have the same form.

Just as a side note, although Boolean arithmetic looks similar to binary arithmetic, Boolean differs from binary in that there are only ever two possible states, 1 or 0, and therefore while 1 + 1 is 10 in binary arithmetic it is 1 in Boolean arithmetic.

There are 16 operations in Boolean algebra but in fact all of them can be synthesised by using combinations of either *not-and* or *not-or* gates. A *not-and* gate is the combination of an *and-gate* with negation. The negation is an additional transistor that simply reverses the output from the *and-gate* so that 0 becomes 1 and 1 becomes 0. In a *not-or* gate the same thing happens with the output from an *or-gate*. The big advantage of this is that it makes manufacture simpler and cheaper, because chip makers only have to make a single type of logic gate.

Shannon's 1938 paper was arguably one of the three significant advances that led to the development of the modern computer. The other two happened around the same time. The first was the development of the theory of computation, which culminated in a paper by Alan Turing published in 1936. The second was the design of the stored program architecture that is used in almost all modern computers, a design originally outlined by John von Neumann in a paper of 1945.

The basic premise of computing won't change if it proves possible to build a quantum computer. An electronic logic gate takes definite inputs and creates a definite output, because the physical system that functions as the base follows an invariable pattern of succession. A quantum logic gate would take definite inputs and create a probabilistic output; therefore, in order to build a quantum logic gate, it will be necessary to position a physical base that follows a probabilistic pattern of succession between inputs and outputs.

What happens when a computer completes an operation is that the representation we understand is translated into binary form. The binary form is then mapped onto the input registers of the computer, the current is switched on, flows through the logic gates and sets the output registers. When an algorithm requires either multiplication or a logical *and*, the flow of electric current is directed through the equivalent of an *and-gate*. When an algorithm requires either addition or a logical *or*, the flow of the electric current is directed through the equivalent of an *or-gate*. The output registers are then mapped back into binary form and this is then translated back into the representation we understand.

The computer itself is just electric current flowing through electronic circuitry, but the flow is controlled so that the state changes in the circuit are a precise analogue of the state changes in the algorithm. In this way meaning reliably persists through the state changes in a physical system.

We can say that an electronic computer is form-holding for computation rather than form-giving, because the state changes in the algorithm drive the state changes in the electronic components. This is possible because the meaning-empty electronic components of the computer can be made to hold a shape that is an analogue of the meaning-full components of the calculation.

It so happens that electronic components can be organised to run computer programs, and are the best way we know at the moment. But any structure with the same formal attributes could function as the hardware. For example, you could take a crowd of people, if you had a suitable crowd, and arrange them on a field, if you had a suitable field, so that each person plays the part of a component in an electronic computer. Each one would be given instructions about which output to signal for any given set of inputs. Communication could be carried out visually by means of flags in a sort of semaphore, so that, for example, 1 might be represented by a yellow flag and 0 by a blue flag. Such a people-in-a-field computer could be made to function, but it would be very slow and unreliable. It would have very poor form-holding properties.

## In search of significance

The signs in the equation 12÷3 = 4 have a meaning, and the ability to reliably complete such computations implies an authentic grasp of that meaning. However, we don't normally attribute an authentic grasp of meaning to a computer, even though computers can reliably complete the calculation, because we understand how the process has been implemented as a mechanism. We know this about computers because we build and program them.

Alan Turing published his paper on the theory of computation in 1936. The theory is based on the idea of the algorithm, which is a method of carrying out state changes in a system. An algorithm is a sequence of instructions that, if completed correctly, will accomplish a task. There is a start instruction and a stop instruction, and a computable process is one that can be completed in a finite number of instructions.

The term 'algorithm' was originally closely connected to algebra and the use of algebraic methods to solve mathematical problems. Both terms came into use in Europe in 1145, in the translation into Latin of a book originally written in 830 in Arabic. Algoritmi was the Latinised form of the name of the writer, Persian mathematician Al-Kwarizmi, and *al-jabr* is the Arabic word for the techniques.

The idea is that tasks can be broken down into a sequence of very simple moves, such that at each step in the process it is only necessary to detect the state of the system and carry out the instruction defined for that state. The simple moves that constitute an algorithm can be completed without whatever is doing the processing having any knowledge of the task of which it is a part or its purpose and significance.

This idea can be applied more widely than computation. Any process that can be broken down into a series of moves, such that each move is as simple as possible and can be carried out without reference to the design and intention of the process as a whole, can be considered algorithmic. The processor in this sense can be a piece of machinery, a person or an organisation. Bureaucratic processes aspire to the condition of the algorithm, as do many industrial processes such as the factory assembly line. Like these processes, computation can be modularised, with processing distributed across replaceable modules that carry out parts of the task, and, in this sense, computation is typical of the engineering models that underlie modern industrial societies.

Computation is necessary to the analogy between meaningful process and physical process on which modern computing is based. Logic gates process inputs at a very fine-grained scale; if it weren't possible to break down computations into equally small units on the same scale, it wouldn't be possible to design an electronic circuit as the physical correlate of an algorithm.

The early attempts to build machine intelligence tended to assume a computational theory of the mind. This is the idea that the mind is, fundamentally, an algorithm processor. Research was guided by the idea that thinking was a process of manipulating information captured in representational symbols according to a set of rules of inference. By the late 1960s this approach had run into insurmountable difficulties. Relatively simple activities turned out to require far more information than was being captured in the abstract conceptual models being used. It turned out that even the simplest course of action might involve many layers of information and functionality. The theorists and engineers had been over-confident, drawing on beliefs that assumed the world is simpler than it actually is.

One prominent critic was Hubert Dreyfus, who argued that research had been too focused on micro-worlds, artificial situations in which the small number of features that were possibly relevant was determined beforehand. In his book *What Computers Can't Do,* which was published in 1972, he argued that human beings are biological systems embedded in social and intellectual contexts. As such, much human thinking is intuitive, informal and situational, and consequently beyond the capabilities of formal rule-following machine intelligence. Human beings have a grasp of things that cannot be captured in a set of rules, or even necessarily be fully represented.

Dreyfus called this 'the problem of significance'. Drawing on Heidegger's concept of the ready-to-hand, he argued that we grasp the world initially in its significance for us. The world we inhabit is not a world of things or even of functions, but rather a world of significances and relevancies:

> *...learning our way around in the world modifies our brain and so builds significance and relevance into the world so that relevance is directly experienced in the way tasks summon us...*

We apprehend a hammer not as form and composition, or even as function, but initially as a tool that will be useful – how does this object help or hinder our construction project? This is what Heidegger meant when he said that the ready-to-hand is prior to the present-at-hand. The question this raised for Dreyfus was, thus, how a machine intelligence could understand significance. What would have relevance for a machine? What could it possibly care about?

One response to the difficulties then being encountered by traditional high concept artificial intelligence research were robotics based not on detached conceptual models that then had to find some application, but a more direct navigation of the environment. Dreyfus called this idea Heideggerian AI. The underlying idea is captured in the rubric, proposed by Rodney Brook, that *the world is its own best map*. Rather than learning an abstract conceptual model and then trying to apply it to the situation at hand, the software learnt a particular environment from the bottom up by attempting to navigate it. But this research program also had only limited success; it never proved possible to scale up beyond or extrapolate from the original environment, and it didn't solve the problem of significance.

In an essay with the formidable title *Why Heideggerian AI Failed and How Fixing It Would Require Making It More Heideggerian*, Dreyfus argued that:

> ...we would also need – and here's the rub – a model of our particular way of being embedded and embodied such that what we experience is significant for us in the particular way that it is. That is, we would have to include in our program a model of a body very much like ours with our needs, desires, pleasures, pains, ways of moving, cultural background, etc.

These philosophical insights with regard to artificial intelligence map well to some recent thinking in neuroscience, for example in the work of Antonio Damasio. Damasio's concept of the homeostatic imperative explains how significance is embedded in the operation of a living organism. The dynamics of homeostasis are the common ground between biological and cultural processes. The homeostatic imperative is the self-sustaining operation of living systems that guides the selection of biological structures capable of maintaining and advancing the evolution of species. Homeostasis operates at all biological scales: cells, organisms and populations.

Damasio places emphasis on the nervous system as a whole-organism system, as are the circulatory, immune and endocrine systems. It is the coordinated functioning of whole-organism systems that make multicellular organisms viable. The nervous system performs a surveillance function in an organism, monitoring the status of each component of the system and engaging a homeostatic response, that is, one that maintains the variables of an internal milieu within a narrow range. The first nervous systems were neural nets capable of responding to events but without the capacity to create an internal model of the world. More sophisticated minds can create internal representations that are able to support the possibility of guided action.

There are two kinds of homeostatic process. There are non-conscious forms of physiological control that can function without minds, and there are forms that require minds that are conscious and have experiences. At this second level, what we experience as feelings are reports concerning the homeostatic status of the organism and the functioning of the organism. Much of the time the ebb and flow of feelings is a background hum but when, for example, we are wounded, the reports from that location, the pain we feel, become sufficiently compelling to ensure the attention of the whole organism. Because an organism feels the world, mental states always have a valence, a judgement about the state of an organism, its well-being or malaise. Significance is in this way built-in to self-sustaining biological entities.

Damasio argues that the basic features of consciousness are that it is integrated, subjective and felt. Consciousness implies both that the internal representation in the mind is integrated with an emotional significance and that it is constructed and interpreted from a point of view. The idea that there is a localised theatre in the mind is an illusion, but it is a necessary and functional illusion constructed out of tricks available to the brain–body partnership;

strategies and mechanisms that have their antecedents deep in the evolution of life.

# Engineering intelligence

At the moment the capabilities of artificial intelligence fall a long way short of human capabilities, but do we interpret this to be a consequence of the immaturity of the technology, or is there some inevitable limit to what can be achieved? As Dreyfus put it, are we starting a journey to the moon, or learning to climb trees?

There are at least two aspects to the problem of significance as an engineering challenge. These might be called the question of mechanical assembly and the question of equipment. The question of mechanical assembly is specifically the question: can a *machine* be constructed that is functionally equivalent to a human being? It wouldn't be surprising if, perhaps as a consequence of the search for extra-terrestrial life, we discovered that another living organism had the same capabilities, but positing them in a machine creates a feeling of anxiety about what it means to be human. It crosses the boundary that divides artefact from nature.

In this context, the limits of machinery are the limits of computation, and computations are scripted processes that require a designer. The significance of this can be brought out by comparing the theory of computation to the theory of evolution in biology. There is both a significant similarity and a significant difference in these models. The similarity is that the molecular machinery in the cell looks like an algorithmic process. The difference is that while algorithmic processes are designed and scripted, biological processes are events in self-sustaining systems.

In the case of biological evolution, the outcome – the distribution of characteristics and traits in the population of living organisms at a moment in time – is the consequence of internal biological processes operating within the constraints imposed by the physical components of which they are constructed and the external ecosystems which the organisms inhabit. As Christopher Alexander put it in the conversation reported by Stewart Brand:

> *In nature you've got very-small-feedback-loop adaption going on, which is why things get to be harmonious.*

This is not a designed harmony, as there is no co-ordination between the internal and external processes, and neither the internal nor the external processes have any forward-looking capability.

Living organisms are components of self-sustaining systems in a way that non-living entities, whether natural or mechanical, aren't. The intuition that only living organisms can be intelligent is therefore also the intuition that only a self-sustaining system can be intelligent. However, being self-sustaining by itself is necessary but not sufficient. Among self-sustaining systems, only living organisms have sufficient stability to support intelligence.

This then raises the question why, among all living organisms, only human beings are introspectively intelligent. If we follow this line of thought, the hypothesis must be that only human beings among all living organisms also have sufficient scale and complexity to start along this path.

If this is plausible then we can understand why the problem of significance has a solution for human beings but not for machines. As a particular self-sustaining entity, there is for us a *particular way of being embedded and embodied such that what we experience is significant for us in the particular way that it is*. How could a machine, which is not a self-sustaining entity, acquire a sense of the significance of the world it is encountering?

The gradient gets steeper. The second part of the critique is the problem of equipment. Computers are tools. To become intelligent, artificial intelligence will have to cross the boundary that separates equipment from agency, a route that is uncharted. It is not only a cognitive test that would be required for success but also a behavioural one. An artificial intelligence would have to successfully negotiate the way of living of an agent. A machine that was functionally equivalent to a human being would have to be able to participate in the forms of living that are equivalent to human society as an authentic and autonomous being subject to ethical constraints and ethical accountability.

In order for an artificial intelligence to gain promotion from equipment to agency there would also need to be a change in the way that human beings interact with it. For example, it would not be possible to use a machine with a level of capabilities similar to a human being in an instrumental manner. Artificial intelligence engineering is primarily focused on building useful tools. A research path that was dedicated to building an entity equivalent to a human being would have to have an entirely different set of ethics and procedures.

From the perspective of the question of equipment, the problem of significance becomes the question of where significance will come from and whose significance it will be? How could a tool acquire autonomy? Agency can only be taken, it cannot be given. The engineers can build and program a computer to carry out a task but they cannot build a computer that will determine its own tasks. This limitation is embedded in the possibilities of computation as an algorithmic process. An algorithm is a set of instructions that completes an already defined task.

I am doubtful that artificial intelligence with a reasonable equivalence to human intelligence is possible, but not because I think that we have a non-physical soul or because there is something inherently mysterious about intelligence. I suspect that it will turn out that constructing an artificial equivalent to a human being is conceivable but not achievable, because there isn't a practical path to artificial intelligence. If authentic intelligence requires organic development rather than mechanical assembly, and is a cultural as well as a biological event, it may be that the only path to authentic intelligence is the one by which we came; the route through millions of years of evolution of biological form and thousands of years of cultural acquisition.

Rules-based artificial intelligence has turned into successful expert system applications that capture a target domain at a level of abstraction that matches the way specialists in the field think. Current research into artificial intelligence has been focused on neural networks. In a neural network program, the processing is organised into a stack. There is an input layer of processors and an output layer of processors, and one or more intermediate layers between them. The basic idea is to create a path between input layer and output layer through the intermediate layers. The path is a series of successive transformations of the input data pattern, until it becomes the output data pattern.

This is somewhat similar in concept to those word games where you are given a four-letter word such as M-I-N-D and your task is to turn it into another four-letter word such as G-A-M-E in five steps such that at each step you can only change one letter and each interim step must form a valid word:

M-I-N-D

M-I-N-E

T-I-N-E

T-I-M-E

T-A-M-E

G-A-M-E

The difference is that in a neural network the data is numeric, the transformations are mathematical operations rather than letter substitutions, and there are many more layers and many more nodes.

Neural networks aren't scripted in the sense that an algorithm is scripted. Neural networks are set up by adjusting the transformations in the intermediate layers. For example, a classification program is presented with sample numeric input patterns that have already been classified, and then the weight given to the mathematical operations in each layer is adjusted until the system reliably connects the input to appropriate output patterns. The program can then be used to sort and classify similar inputs.

A second type of neural network is called an auto-encoder. In this case the inputs to the program aren't classified. The idea is that if the software can generate, as output, patterns appropriate to the unclassified input, it can be taken to have worked out what the salient features of the input were. Here is how Paul Taylor, in an update on the state of play in the *London Review of Books*, describes the problem:

> *The challenge in machine learning is not so much finding a rule that correctly classifies a particular set of data, as finding the rule that is most likely to work for future examples. One approach that would work for a linearly separable problem would be to divide the two sets using the straight line that maximises the distance between the line and the nearest point in each of the two sets. Finding that line is mathematically relatively straightforward. But the most interesting problems tend not to lend themselves to linear separation. A mathematically elegant solution is to project*

> *the data into a higher dimensional space where a simple separation can be found by a process of iterative searching.*

This higher dimensional space is called a feature space. The feature space has to be sufficiently multi-dimensional that every combination of relevant differentiating criteria is given a distinct location in the feature space. A two-dimensional space is adequate if a line can be drawn between the relevant data points. Similarly, a three-dimensional volume will work if it is then possible to insert a plane to separate the instances. For multi-dimensional spaces the equivalent is a hyperplane. and it is the problem of working out how to build a feature space that allows the separation of the inputs by a hyperplane that research in pattern recognition and classification is trying to solve.

The breakthrough in pattern recognition applications came when it was realised that an auto-encoder could be used to work out the optimum feature space for inputs such as normal speech. A standard neural network could then use the output from the auto-encoder to sort and classify the information. In a many-layered neural network, the lower layers derive the optimum feature space and the upper layers do the classification. Paul Taylor continues in his article:

> *Geoffrey Hinton, one of a dwindling number of researchers still working on neural networks, realised that if the lower levels of a neural network could be programmed using autoencoders, then the bottom of a deep neural network could learn a feature space that the top of the network could*

> use to perform a classification. In 2009 two of Hinton's students used this approach to devise a speech recognition system which was, within a few years of development, outperforming competitors that had been refined for thirty years or more.

Neural networks differ from scripted algorithms to the extent that the sequence of moves that accomplishes a task is not determined beforehand and may be opaque to the developers. For this reason, it also doesn't have to be representational. Although the derived feature space must be an analogue of a conceptual representation, it doesn't have to be limited to anything that a human being could intuitively understand.

Computers running scripted algorithms can complete the same tasks that a human being can complete but more quickly and more reliably. That is basically why we use them. It may be possible to build neural networks that accomplish pattern recognition and classification tasks not only as well as human beings can, but even better. There is no reason to suppose that human being's intuitive capabilities are at the limit of what is possible.

This has given rise to renewed anxiety regarding the possibility that artificial intelligence might surpass human intelligence, but I think these anxieties are misplaced. Neural networks don't change the fundamental nature of computation: computers remain pieces of equipment that are assembled mechanically and that accomplish tasks that have been defined for them. We're still climbing trees, not shooting for the moon.

That is not to say that there is no cause for concern about the use of computers in human society. However, the cause for concern lies more in the nature of algorithmic computation and its similarity to bureaucratic and industrial processes. Done well, modern forms of organisation are hugely beneficial to humanity; done badly, they become a blight. There exists the possibility that the implementation of computational technology will reduce human beings to algorithm processors, limited to recognising which move to make but not allowed to be concerned with the purpose or significance of the course of action of which they have become a component.

## Introspection and consciousness

There is a set of capabilities that are unique to human beings, at least as far as we know for now, because, given the size of the universe, there must be a fair possibility that there are similar beings elsewhere. This package of capabilities, which might be called introspective intelligence, includes language, an ability to grasp abstract ideas detached from context, the ability to complete a cultural performance, foresight, ethical accountability and a sense of self. Intuitively, because they appear together and, when they do appear at all they appear together, it seems reasonable to start from an assumption that these capabilities are interdependent.

We usually assume that animals are conscious but lack the capacity for introspection. This distinction between consciousness and introspection isn't always carefully drawn and the terms are often used interchangeably. But the importance of the distinction can be gauged by thinking about Julian Jaynes' theory of the bicameral mind. Jaynes argued that the capacity for introspection appears very late in human evolution, occurring after the invention of written language and perhaps little more than 3,200 years ago, at least in Europe and the Middle East, during a period that is sometimes called the Bronze Age Collapse.

In outline the theory is as follows. Introspection is a learned process that is dependent on the possession of metaphorical language. It is not simply a biological event. While we are aware of at least some of our own thinking and can reflect on it, the bicameral mind was not aware of its own deliberations. Decision-making happened below the level of conscious awareness. The outcome of the unconscious process of deliberation, the decision about what course of action to take, was heard as a command communicated by the right side to the left side of the bicameral mind. These auditory illusions were attributed to the gods or to the rulers or to dead ancestors. The rationale for doing something couldn't be articulated, because the reasoning process was hidden below the level of awareness in much the same way that we aren't conscious of the mechanism by which our visual systems serve images to the mind. Jaynes suggests that the command hallucinations heard by people suffering from schizophrenia are vestiges of this earlier organisation of the mind.

In the theory, the auditory commands that communicate decisions about what to do in the face of new circumstances are the outcome of a deliberation in a particular context, mediated through language, which draws upon culturally acquired resources. In sufficiently uncomplicated situations the bicameral mind could arrive without introspection at similar conclusions to those that a self-aware mind working within the same cultural framework of information and ideas would come to. However, this kind of mental functioning was inadequate to deal with the increasing complexity of society, particularly at a time of disruption, and this led to the evolution of unitary consciousness and the awareness of awareness.

Jaynes' theory draws evidence from psychology and neuroscience, and the analysis of early poems such as the *Iliad*. From a cultural perspective, placing the transition to the introspective mind around 3,200 years ago seems somewhat late in the day. Anatomically modern humanity is thought to have evolved by about 190,000 years ago, and behaviourally modern humanity sometime before 40,000 years ago. The cultural acquisition that had occurred by 3,200 years ago already included significant complexity: agriculture, cities, writing, accounting, poetry, painting, bureaucracy, contracts, states, trade and warfare. Is it really possible that the state bureaucracies, written record keeping and technological innovation of Egypt and Mesopotamia could have happened without anyone in the population having some capacity for self-awareness and introspection? Did the movement of peoples around the Mediterranean 3,200 years ago really represent an unprecedented step change in both complexity and disruption?

Part of the difficulty with the theory is trying to imagine what it would mean to lack this kind of awareness. Much of our thinking is intuitive and, as it were, automated, particularly when we are occupied by routine tasks. This lack of attention is usually because routine tasks are being accomplished in the background while typically something more introspective is happening in the foreground. However, this doesn't really evoke an experience in which there is only background and no foreground.

The nearest I can get is to imagine some sort of dream-like state: a shared coherent dreaming rather than our private, often incoherent, dreams, and without the flooding in of awareness that happens when we are in the process of waking up. But what I like about the theory is that it puts into play something we might otherwise never think clearly about. There must have been some such transition or awakening, if not when Jaynes places it and through the mechanism that he suggests, then at another time and in some other way. We shouldn't assume that the capacity for introspection is just a biological event.

One aspect of this distinction between consciousness and introspection is the question of what each cares about. A shift from consciousness to introspection would also involve a shift in motivations. Conscious beings are living systems and inherit the self-sustaining functioning of living systems. A conscious being cares about its well-being in the environment in which it finds itself. But a conscious being is not aware of itself as a separate entity. It lacks interiority.

Introspective beings are also conscious beings and living systems and inherit the same self-sustaining functioning, but an introspective being is aware of its interiority and therefore of the distinction between inside and outside. What is being sustained is not just the living organism in its environment but also the separateness and the coherence of the internal experience.

The introspective experience of living is generally recognised by both supporters and opponents as an area of weakness for all forms of philosophical naturalism. While the exclusion from science of the subject of cognizance, which Erwin Schrödinger called the opening gambit, is operationally a strength for the practice of science it is also, inevitably, a liability for any naturalistic philosophy grounded in the scientific world picture.

While I think this criticism is justified, it is fair to add that this weakness is not specific to philosophical naturalism. This is because the problem originates in the reductive insistence on a single layer of explanation. The same objection applies to not only to scientific materialism but also to panpsychism, natural teleology and every other non-materialist version of reductivism. Thomas Nagel, for example, points to the problems in *Mind and Cosmos* but doesn't offer an alternative solution.

Furthermore, for the same reason, positing a separate domain of *mind* doesn't really help. Suppose for a moment that there exists as part of the cosmos a domain that is not observable by science and cannot be understood in terms of physics, chemistry and biology; would an understanding of the nature of conscious and introspective awareness suddenly become apparent? Like the theories that posit an extra-terrestrial origin for life, dualist theories of mind relocate the problem, they do not resolve it.

We don't really have an idea of what it means to be an observer of rather than a participant in the world at all. It may be there isn't a further explanation, something else in terms of which experience is explicable. However, I think the distinction between participant and observer is a better way of thinking about consciousness and introspection than using the ideas of mind and matter. I suggest that instead of asking how a collection of molecules can originate introspective and intelligent minds, we should ask what it means to be an observer and what it means to be a participant, and build a model of observation and participation that can then be mapped back into our scientific models.

What does it mean to be a spectator rather than a participant? Although the defining metaphor of a model he opposes, Daniel Dennett's image of a Cartesian theatre in the mind is apt. Our term 'theatre' comes from the Greek word *'theatron'*, meaning 'to behold', and is closely linked to the term 'theory', which derives from *'theoros'*, meaning 'spectator'. To see and to think is to take on the role of spectator, to become an observer in the universe. The role of spectator at a performance doesn't include any contributions that change the state of the performance. Spectators are simply observers and not participants. The defining characteristic of a spectator is separation from the flow of events, just as the defining characteristic of a participant is to be caught up them. A spectator is detached from the evolution of events around them. Being a spectator is also a process, a flow of events, but the observing system and the observed system are separated, and there is a shearing layer between them.

This supports the idea that observers can only exist at the macro-scale, because it is only at this scale that there can be a separation of objects and persons. At the micro-scale there are only the processes of physics and chemistry. The boundaries between separate entities with which we are ordinarily familiar at the macro-scale are, at most, only dotted lines at the level of physics and chemistry, and events flow freely across these boundaries.

At the micro-scale, there isn't the possibility of the detachment required for there to be observers in the universe.

## Intelligence and cultural performances

One of the advantages of approaching the problem in this way and separating consciousness from introspection is that it avoids simple mind–body dichotomies.

Intelligence is not a well-defined concept. In many uses it is defined quite narrowly, in terms of effective cognitive abilities. I have been using it to mean something quite wide: the ability to participate in a cultural performance. Some of these performances are scripted, others improvised. My view is that if we want to think seriously about intelligence, it is these kinds of capabilities we need to be thinking about; intelligence as the capacity to engage in a cultural performance, and the measure of intelligence as the scope and extent of the performances to which this capacity is the gateway.

One of the reasons that intelligence is difficult to define is that it isn't a single system but a set of capacities. These capabilities come in interrelated clusters rather than as discrete items. There are, I suggest, at least three clusters: the first is concerned with navigation, communication, and consciousness; the second is concerned with language, abstract thought and cultural acquisition; and the third is concerned with introspection, the sense of self and ethical accountability.

The first set of capabilities is oriented towards navigation, communication and consciousness. There is a map of the terrain to navigate by, but it is a low-concept, rough-and-ready map constructed according to the principle that *the world is its own best map*. For a living organism, the role of the nervous system is surveillance, integration and the co-ordination of operations. It is a system for observation, co-ordination and response. Navigation doesn't require the highly conceptual models that become available through language and cultural acquisition. Navigational maps aren't abstractions from conceptual maps. The map is environment-specific and optimised for navigation through the terrain while avoiding the hazards it contains.

Navigational maps come informed by significance. What gets into the map is what is significant for the organism: what it cares about and, we may suppose, what cares about it. The map contains information about what is harmful and what is helpful. This means that it already contains a set of orientations, because navigational maps are built out of significances. These significances are not simply cognitive but are mediated through multiple systems within the organism. This was Dreyfus's argument: navigation without significance is inert; navigation must be informed by a particular way of being.

At this level there is consciousness and communication rather than self-awareness and language. Consciousness and communication are closely linked. Consciousness is existence as a receiver of messages, while communication implies a capacity to be also a sender of messages. This raises the question: at what level does incoming information become a message? I think the answer is when it becomes a cue or prompt rather than a trigger.

Simple organisms sense and respond to information about their state and the state of the environment, but in simple organisms there is no detachment from the process. Consciousness is the level of being at which straight-through processing of information from the internal and external environment is interrupted in the internal machinery of the mind, and, conversely, the internal functioning of the mind is interrupted by information from inside and outside itself that requires a response.

The second set of capabilities is defined by the acquisition of language and culture. The possession of language functions as a constraint on the possibility of grasping abstract concepts, the storage and transmission of cultural artefacts, and the repetition of cultural performances. An intelligent being has all the resources of language to open up the conceptual space for a complex set of cultural performances. As well as navigating the physical environment, an intelligent being navigates a conceptual landscape.

Language is a level of communication that is not tethered in space and time to the here and now but can be applied to events in the past and the future, anytime or no-time, elsewhere, anywhere and nowhere. This capacity for displacement is one of the features that distinguishes language from communication. The detachment that language makes possible frees the mind, giving entry to a conceptual and imagined domain not limited to the demands that come with being a living organism.

Language makes possible the capacity for abstraction and analogy that allows the construction of conceptual models. The guiding rubric at this level is *the map is not the territory*. Conceptual space is far more expansive than actual space, extending beyond what is experienced to what can be inferred and imagined, and exploration of this terrain can be guided beyond the self-sustaining imperative of a living organism. At this level the maps are abstract, conceptual and general purpose.

The capacity for introspection is the central component of the third cluster. It's difficult to see how there can be the possibility of ethical accountability without there being a sense of self, and it's difficult to see how there can be a sense of self without there being a capacity for introspection. Equally, it's difficult to see how a capacity for introspection can be sustained without at the same time generating a sense of self and the requirement for ethical accountability. The experience of introspection is grounded in the separateness of persons, and the characteristics of the self that are discovered in introspection are its separateness and its singleness. It may also be the case that our sense of ourselves as single and separate is a creation of our capacity for introspection.

The corollary of interiority is a separation of what is inward looking and internal from what is outward looking and external. The interiority that introspection creates requires the detachment that comes with separation, and therefore relies on the possibility of a separation between inner and outer. Intuitively, this very basic but highly conceptual distinction requires the resources of language to bring it into focus.

The experience of interiority is not just of detachment from the external but also detachment from the internal. We experience the external world as an observer and, when we reflect introspectively, we experience our own interiority as an observer. But the state of being an observer is elusive. We can detach ourselves from and override our emotions, and we can detach ourselves from and override our intuitive mind. But we cannot detach ourselves from our introspective self. We cannot observe ourselves as observers. As soon as we try to capture our inner self in the activity of thinking it eludes us, the thought spinning away to become part of the observed world.

Introspection is awareness of an internal world separate from the external world. It is also the experience of this internal world as a private space to which only we have access. We share the external world, we don't share our internal worlds. In this way, introspection is necessary for our sense of ourselves and the basis of agency. Ethical accountability has to be carried by a single separate self-aware entity that recognises itself as the source of its own actions. There is no acceptance of agency in a situation where the responsibility for a course of action is unreflective or projected onto a god, a ruler or a dead ancestor.

Although introspection is awareness of an inner system that we think of as *me*, we don't have to assume that this is especially privileged access. We may wonder how much we, the introspective self, are actually in control of the system. Like the captain on the bridge of a ship, most of the time things seem to happen more or less as we expect them to, but we don't organise operations or necessarily know much about how the process is working in detail.

One aspect of this is that the introspective experience is as much, perhaps even more, a unity in time as it is in space. What is intuitive and what is introspective isn't fixed but shifts over time. What is practiced and habitual drops below the level of introspective attention, while what is unpractised and unexpected occupies our self-awareness. What was once introspective becomes intuitive. It is only from the perspective of continuity through time that we can recognise that the way the system functions now is the consequence of the experience accumulated and the decisions made over a lifetime.

The advantage of such a model is that it accommodates and manages the tension between two demands: on the one hand, the need for an account that contains the continuity in the evolution of life that reaches from the simplest to the most complex living organisms and locates human experience within that continuity; and on the other, the need for an account that contains the discontinuity that is the basis of human exceptionalism and the possibility of language, culture and intelligence.

I don't mean to imply that there cannot be any other authentic modes of being intelligent. The limits of conceptual thinking in language are not the limits of knowledge and therefore, by the same logic, we can imagine that the ground we traverse in conceptual thinking, a different kind of intelligence might traverse in a quite different manner.

In his study of cephalopod intelligence, *Other Minds*, Peter Godfrey-Smith makes a similar argument:

> *But it [language] is not essential to the organisation of ideas, and language is not the medium of complex thought.*
>
> *I'd resist the idea that higher-order thought is the essential step that brings us to the kind of experience seen in humans. It's one piece of the story, though it may be an especially important part. Perhaps the most vivid of all forms of conscious thought are those in which we bring attention to bear on our own thought processes, reflect on them, and experience them as our own. We can look in at our own internal states without thinking in words about them, but in the undeniable Why-did-I-think-that? or Why-did-I-feel-that-way? cases of consciousness, inner speech is prominent.*

A useful analogy might be drawn with locomotion. Bipedalism, walking and running on two legs, is not the only way of getting about, but it is humanity's predominant method, and the opportunities and constraints bipedalism imposes are part of what defines the human predicament. Similarly, conceptual thinking mediated through language may not be the only way in which to be introspectively intelligent, but it is the predominant way for human minds, and the opportunities made possible and the constraints imposed by thinking conceptually fundamentally shape the human experience.

One of the best test cases for any account of introspective intelligence is ethical accountability, because only authentically introspective intelligence draws ethical accountability. This doesn't mean that ethics is disconnected from the evolution of living organisms. The picture contains that continuity. But an introspective intelligence will inevitably become aware of questions of rationality, legitimacy and authenticity that a merely conscious organism, however sophisticated, will never have to face. Ethical accountability is in this way a component of the predicament of an introspective being.

CHAPTER FIVE

# ACTION AND PRACTICAL REASONING

## Objectives, strategies and constraints

In 5th century Athens the term *'strategos'* referred to a general, who could be either a military or a political leader, and the term *'strategia'* meant the office that they held and the expertise that they practised. They were responsible both for raising forces and deploying them in the field. There were normally ten at a time, and they held office for a year. In modern usage the derived term *strategist* has a looser application, indicating a role rather than an office, but it has the same broad meaning.

The role of a strategist is to plan the application of a set of resources towards the attainment of a set of objectives within a set of limitations or constraints. Objectives, strategies and constraints can be viewed as the components of a simple conceptual model of action, one in which a course of action is conceptualised as a project.

I don't mean to imply by this that every course of action is a project. Actions must often respond to events that are foreseeable only in part, and sometimes not at all, and any account of action should be able to comprehend both the routine and the wayward, the unreflective and the unexamined. We shouldn't impose an unjustified consistency or rationality on behaviour. In this case the idea of the project serves as a prototype. Rather than getting lost trying to track the complexity of actual behaviour with an equally complex model, the application of a simple model makes it possible to understand the complexity by looking at how reality is at variance with the model. This is particularly an advantage in the case, as it often is, where the diversity is the consequence of absences, things that aren't there rather than things that are. What does the absence of objectives and strategy in a course of action tell us?

Strategies are determined by objectives and constraints. An objective is a goal to be achieved, something to be attained or to be avoided, and a strategy is the method of achieving or avoiding it. Objectives are usually organised into structures rather than being determined in isolation. Typically, a small set of organisational objectives will be broken down into a number of more manageable project objectives. There is also likely to be a set of tactical objectives designed to adapt project and organisational strategies to the course of events. Tactical and project objectives inherit at least a part of their purpose from the large-scale organisational objectives.

An objective doesn't necessarily have to be an end state; a goal may be defined in other terms, such as positioning or momentum. To function as an objective, an outcome must also be reasonably specific, although reasonableness here is a graduated dimension. Tactical objectives are usually defined more precisely, because a vaguely specified tactical objective would have only limited value. Project objectives should be well enough defined to guide decision-making without being overly sensitive to the inevitable turbulence in a course of events. Organisational objectives, on the other hand, can be specified in broader terms because their function is architectural. A set of high-level organisational goals creates a framework that allows us to order and organise projects, to communicate progress and measure success and failure.

Formal objectives may not be functional objectives. There are situations where the performance of the strategy rather than the achievement of the objectives is the motivation. The desired outcome can be a framing device, in the way that we might define a destination in order to make a journey, where the experience of the journey rather than reaching the destination is the primary purpose. This is most likely to be the case with overarching goals. How are very high-level organisational objectives determined? The ideas we use to describe ultimate objectives aren't sufficiently well defined to be specific end-states to be reached, but more background states, a means of framing ideas about a better way of living: justice, liberty, peace, truth, prosperity, recognition, happiness, knowledge and so on.

A course of action is a component of a course of events. Most events are not actions; they are the patterns of adjustment, accommodation and adaptation that occur in the evolution of the world. A course of action is woven into a course of events in the way the threads in a rope are woven together. Actions both respond to and shape the course of events.

Because there is always a course of events, it follows that doing nothing is a form of doing something; inaction is effectively an action. We cannot choose to step away from the course of events; all we can do is exercise some influence over the shape the course of events takes. We are always making headway. Kierkegaard describes this idea using the image of a ship's captain:

> *Think of the captain on his ship at the instant when it has to come about. He will perhaps be able to say, 'I can either do this or that'; but… he will be aware at the same time that the ship is all the while making its usual headway, and that therefore it is only an instant when it is indifferent whether he does this or that.*

The failure to act is an action because the course of events doesn't stand still, waiting for us to come to a decision, but flows on, turning the absence of any decision into a decision. If we fail to act, we will be carried along by the current, and our course of action will be one that has been determined for us and not one we have determined for ourselves. The implication of this is that we don't need to have a coherent set of purposes and goals, reasons, intentions and motivations in order to act, because making a move cannot be avoided. There must always be a move and it must always be now. But this necessity is only that there should be some move, not that it should be this or that particular move.

This is the predicament we discover as we grow up and become aware that we are participants in a performance that is already in progress. We became protagonists before we knew there was a role. There is no initial position before the first move is made during which we have the time to make plans, work out objectives or devise a strategy, and there will be no opportunities to call for a time-out to gather our thoughts.

There is a multi-layered structure to a course of action. The architecture is governed by the structuring of time and the layering is a reflection of scale and the pace of change. At the largest scale, our lives are shaped by significant organising decisions that are made and remade only a few times during a lifetime. These structuring decisions create the framework that orders and constrains smaller scale projects and habitual and routine actions. The large-scale story unfolds over the long term and is likely to change only slowly, if at all, while short-term habitual and routine actions are made and remade continually and have limited ramifications. At the middle scale, there are the particular projects we engage in.

This doesn't have to be a hierarchical model, although it may be. For example, the activities of a working day may be, all at the same time, the repetition of routine and habitual bureaucracy, tasks to complete as part of a project, and a moment in the evolution of the organisation. But it's likely that there will be many projects in play at the same time, overlapping and intersecting, and many routine and habitual actions will not belong to any project. The model I have in mind is the idea that every action is a transformation of the state of the system as a whole.

This partitioning of actions by scale and the pace of change creates shearing layers. The structure must allow slippage between the differently paced layers. The slow-moving institutional layers must be sufficiently flexible to adapt to and accommodate the flow of actions and events, but at the same time sufficiently resilient to persist through the constant turnover and turbulence of the fast-moving transactional layers.

There are two processes required to shape a course of action. The first process is deliberation. This is where the participants identify their objectives and constraints and work out their strategies. It isn't only individuals who must turn their intentions into decisions in a process of deliberation; the same processes apply to deliberative councils. Committees, courts, boards and parliaments are all engaged in deliberations, and most institutions in most societies are governed by a deliberative council of some kind.

The second process is negotiation. This is where the participants discuss, debate and bargain in order to determine which courses of action are actually going to happen. Deliberation is a monologue, whereas negotiation is a dialogue, sometimes a crowd scene. The techniques of deliberation are the means by which we form objectives and create strategies, and the techniques of negotiation are the means by which we bargain with other participants to determine the actual course of action that will be taken.

Negotiation is also the time when we collect obligations. Agreements, promises, contracts, exchanges, loans and commitments are the unavoidable consequence of sharing the terrain. There is also, I think, an obligation that arises simply because we do share the terrain, the obligation to participate in good faith.

Although distinct in concept and techniques, these two processes intersect and usually run concurrently. It's possible they may happen in sequence but typically our deliberations will reflect our negotiating position, and our negotiating position will reflect our deliberations. What usually happens is that we shuttle between deliberation and negotiation in a process of continual adjustment, accommodation and adaptation.

All negotiations have some component of bargaining and some component of institution building. Bargaining is primarily transactional; the attempt to work out the terms of a specific trade, and the parties to the transaction may not have many other interests in common except that they will benefit from the trade. But even the most transactional of exchanges is usually carried out with some sense that by successfully completing the transaction, the practice of bargaining and the relationship between the parties is strengthened, which implies some element of institution building and maintenance.

Public institutions, businesses and households can all be seen as the outcomes of bargains, but bargains where the transaction isn't a specific trade but rather the creation of an institutional framework within which future actions can be deliberated and negotiated, where differences can be accommodated and conflicts managed. Because we share the world, we have to have strategies for co-ordination and conflict management. We are engaged in a constant resistance to fraud, violence, intimidation and exploitation. At the largest scale the outcome of these bargains is the system of states and international organisations.

This institution building serves also to place constraints on the course of actions and events. In modern industrialised societies there are typically three patterns of social organisation: networks, bureaucratic hierarchies and communal structures. Civil society and the economy are networks of relationships; government and business organisations are usually bureaucratic hierarchies; and households are typically more communal organisations. In traditional agrarian societies the structures are often more complex and are likely to be organised around the idea of a station-in-life; a position and role in society defined by, among other things, class, caste, family, gender and age. These stations-in-life are typically organised into hierarchies.

These patterns are sufficient to create a course of routine and habitual actions that can completely account for all the time available – a set of constraints sufficiently closely drawn that no self-consciously articulated objectives and strategies are necessary. In the worst situations, circumstances can be so hard and circumscribed that surviving – that is, simply being able to make another move – is the limit of what is possible.

## The heuristics of practical reasoning

How do we determine a set of objectives, strategies and constraints? There are two unavoidable challenges: complexity and incommensurability. The set of possible choices must be sufficiently simple to be manageable, and the decision-making procedure must be able to sensibly evaluate incommensurable options.

Simplification is the first basic challenge of decision-making. Before we can assess the options, it is necessary to simplify the scenarios and reduce unmanageable complexity down to something manageable. To make decision-making manageable, objectives and strategies have to be significantly constrained. There are an almost infinite number of lives that anyone can live. A game of chess is highly constrained, but there are in the order of $10^{120}$ possible courses a game might take. I doubt anyone has even tried to do the calculation for a human life. This isn't necessarily the experience of course; it can often seem as though there are too few choices rather than too many, the habitual and routine too dominant, too intractable.

How do we move from the unmanageably open-ended and undefined to the manageably contained and defined? There are a number of channels through which these simplifications are achieved. These methods are heuristic. As Daniel Kahnmann describes it in *Thinking Fast and Slow, a heuristic is a simple procedure that helps find adequate, though often imperfect, answers to difficult questions.* We use heuristics because we have to make risk-carrying decisions on the basis of limited information, and in a limited time.

Perhaps the most straightforward approach to simplification is to use what might be called an 'evolutionary heuristic'. We typically don't think everything through from scratch each time we make a decision. Instead, we use a copy with variation method to create a manageable decision field. In each cycle of decision-making our choices and preferences are largely those carried forward from the previous cycle, with some relatively small modifications and adjustments. Innovation is incremental and at the margins. We incorporate successful innovations into the baseline that we carry forward to the next cycle, while at the same time discarding other courses of action that are no longer wanted or applicable. This is an evolutionary rather than an optimisation procedure, because we don't attempt to review our decisions globally.

This is the advantage to banality. Simplification is achieved successfully through a strategy of habituation and familiarisation. We hide the complexity, and, because innovation is at the margins, it can be speculative or impulsive and unreflective without creating large risks. On the other side, the disadvantage of an evolutionary approach is that it can also be difficult to change track if the banality is unsatisfactory. It is too easy to get stuck in a course of routine and habitual actions or just float with the current, wayward and purposeless.

A second simplifying heuristic is the way we partition our mental accounting. There isn't a single set of decisions, but rather a number of layers of decision-making at different scales and with different durations. This partitioning is likely to align to the different levels of objectives. At one end of the scale are the significant and long-term organisational decisions that determine the course of our lives and that we make and re-make maybe only once or twice in a lifetime. At the other end of the scale there is tactical decision-making, the multitude of routine and habitual choices we make every day that have limited ramifications. Somewhere in between will be the particular projects we are engaged in. This partitioning by scope and scale simplifies the process of decision-making, because it means that all the day-to-day decision-making is constrained by project structures that change only infrequently, and organisational structures that change rarely, if at all.

The second basic challenge for decision-making is to make choices between incommensurable alternatives. Few of the judgements we have to make are straightforward comparisons of like for like. There are multiple dimensions to incommensurability. Firstly, there is the range of decisions that have to be made across every aspect of human experience. Secondly, options tend to come as bundles and packages, rather than it being possible to select individually, à la carte as it were. Thirdly, there are the inevitable assessments of probability and the value of time; the difficulties of balancing the future against the present and the uncertain against the likely.

Every choice contains a decision about the value of time. We have a subjective sense of the relative significance of the short term and the long term. The value of time is closely connected to the questions of likelihood and the uncertainty of outcomes. The long term is also the most uncertain and therefore potentially where the greatest risk is. But, as Keynes nearly said, the long term may never happen. Our subjective sense of time, uncertainty and risk isn't static, but it is sufficiently stable to be considered a component of an individual's character and a society's culture.

The heuristics of incommensurability are primarily heuristics of discovery. Deliberation is not a process in which we work out what we want; it is a process in which we decide what course of action we are going to take. However, in the process of determining what action we are going to take, we will discover or clarify what it is that we want, which may not be what we thought it was. Actions are sensitive to context, and therefore our motivations and purposes are brought into question as the costs and trade-offs required are modified in the processes of deliberation.

Similarly, negotiation functions to test objectives as much as it is part of the process for their achievement. Negotiation is also part of the heuristics of discovery. It is sometimes only at the moment when we actually have to trade something that we find out its true value for us. The prospect of an exchange tells us something important about how we value things, something we might not otherwise know.

Because of these fundamental levels of incommensurability, practical reasoning is rarely purely puzzle solving. A puzzle is a problem for which there is a known solution, and the task is to work out what that solution is. The purpose of practical reasoning is not typically to find the solution, the objectively correct answer, to a problem. The purpose is usually more to put our thoughts in order and discover what it is that we really value, and from there we can come to understand the right decision.

The process is a mirror we hold up to ourselves. Of course, we can be mistaken about what we value, and we aren't always lucid or honest with ourselves. The goal is to build a model that can be applied to the situation to guide our decision-making. We will normally have an intuitive sense of what the right answer will look like, and the model should confirm our intuitions. If the model contradicts our instincts and our gut feelings, we will probably go back and try to work out the source of the discrepancy: is the model wrong, or is the model showing us something we don't want to see?

Practical reasoning is the process of making sensible decisions about objectives, strategies and constraints faced with an unmanageable complexity and incommensurability. How is this done? Much modern theorising about decision-making is based on the concept of utility. The idea of utility is the attempt to capture the subjective usefulness of things as a quantity on a single scale, and utility optimisation is probably the most common way in modern theorising to try to meet the challenge of incommensurability.

Utility was initially developed in the 18th century in a discipline called psychophysics, as an attempt to try to solve the puzzle of the subjective usefulness of things. It is a psychological quantity. In the language of game theory, utility is the psychological pay-off that comes from the outcome of a course of action. The idea is that if everything can be assigned a utility, then it should be possible to make a like-for-like comparison between the psychological pay-offs from any set of options.

In the form of the expected utility hypothesis developed by John von Neumann and Oskar Morgenstern in 1953, agents faced with a choice of outcomes are assumed to have a set of rational preferences based on their values and beliefs. The idea is that a utility function can be constructed by assigning a numeric value to each outcome. This value represents its subjective usefulness, and the rational decision is therefore to act to bring about the outcome with the highest utility. There are more sophisticated versions of decision theory based on utility, such as the prospect theory that was developed by Daniel Kahneman with Amos Tversky, but they share the basic approach and have the same limitations.

There are a number of problems with this model as a technique for decision-making. First of all, a considerable amount of thought and effort is required in order to arrive at a set of rational preferences that meet the required constraints. Rational decision-making depends on there being a complete and consistent set of preferences, but the model has little to say about how this is to be achieved. This means that the principal challenges of practical reasoning, simplification and incommensurability, have to be overcome before the model can be used.

Secondly, it is debatable whether the constraints are actually achievable. Partly this is a question of the time and information available, and partly a question of the open-endedness of practical decision-making. The theory assumes a defined framework of preferences and outcomes. However, firstly, we may not know enough about the situation or ourselves to form a complete and consistent set of preferences; and secondly, the set of possible outcomes is not fixed but can be varied in the processes of deliberation and negotiation. The model is not well adapted to the fluidity and opacity of the real world.

A third weakness is that utility theory regards rationality as the degree of consistency of actions with preferences, and preferences with each other. But there is nothing that insists that rational consistency in this sense is either possible or desirable. There is no reason to suppose that our values and beliefs can be organised into a single set of consistent preferences and, if this isn't the case, imposing this requirement can only distort the decision-making process. Furthermore, the world is complicated, multi-layered and unpredictable, and pursuing contradictory strategies that recognise this complexity is arguably likely to be more successful than a strategy of seeking an artificial consistency.

The original hope for psychophysics was that psychological quantities would map in some systematic way to physical quantities, and the development of the idea has been driven by the attempt to determine how that mapping might work. Monetary value is the most obvious quantity in this context, but what was clear from the beginning was that price and value aren't the same thing. The relationship between the price of something and its subjective usefulness isn't linear. The fundamental weakness is that, although it is not money, utility is money-shaped. However, money is an interesting and unusual commodity; most commodities are not like money, and the things we care most about are not commodities.

Utilitarian ethics was originally an attempt to build a normative ethical theory that would apply the concept of utility to ethical obligations and accountability. In economics and decision theory, utility is an attempt to quantify usefulness, but usefulness remains a subjective judgement in these fields. A utility function applies only to one person's preferences at one moment in time and in one concrete situation. Similarly, in economics the utility of a commodity is its subjective utility to someone in particular. Utility is posited to underlie an individual's demand for a commodity: we buy things because they will be useful to us. There are many buyers in a market with many different motivations, and while the resulting demand in a market can be aggregated, the underlying utilities can't. In practice, because utility cannot be observed directly and can only ever be inferred from demand, its own usefulness as a concept is doubtful.

Utilitarian ethics, on the other hand, was based on the premise that utility can be observed directly and can and should be aggregated. This implied that it must be possible to construct a utility function for a population. For obvious reasons, the objections that apply to utility as a technique for private decision-making apply with amplified force to utility as a technique for public decision-making. Furthermore, there is also the question of what political structure could legitimately implement this approach. What institutions might represent the virtual person required by utilitarian ethics? It can't be representative democracy, which starts from the assumption that each person is a principal and is designed to navigate and accommodate the incommensurable priorities, interests and values in a population. Perhaps for these reasons, utilitarianism today has become more a theory about whether it is possible to make judgements of value through instrumental reasoning than a normative ethical theory.

A better approach to decision-making, and one that is closer to how we actually come to decisions, is to apply an ordering principle. The basic idea here is that the alternative options are ranked by one criterion, and only if they are equal is a second criterion considered. Instead of ordering the available courses of action directly, as you would do to construct a utility function, an ordering principle is concerned with evaluating the decision criteria.

For example, the medals table at the Olympic Games is constructed using an ordering principle: the number of gold medals won decides the order, then the number of silver medals if the gold medals are tied, and the bronze models if the silver medals are tied. The ordering reflects the objective value of the medals and doesn't require any subjective interpretations of their value. However, the example illustrates a disadvantage of the method, which is that a single gold will trump any number of other medals. As a method of evaluation, therefore, applying an ordering principle may mean that criteria lower down the order are given too little weight.

To make the technique more sophisticated and a better reflection of the way we actually make decisions, we need to add the concept of a threshold and distinguish between constraints and decisive criteria. A threshold is a limit. Consider the Olympic team. Suppose the Sports Ministry, which controls the funding, sets a threshold for success at 10 medals. Which is now the best outcome from three cases A, B and C. In case A, the team wins 8 medals: 4 gold, 2 silver and 2 bronze. In case B, the team wins 10 medals: 2 gold, 3 silver and 5 bronze. In case C the team wins 14 medals: 2 gold, 2 silver and 12 bronze. The answer is that without the Ministry's threshold A is the best outcome followed by B and then C; with the threshold it is B, then C, then A.

The use of thresholds allows us to distinguish between constraints and decisive criteria. In this example, the evaluation criteria are firstly the total number of medals, followed by the number of golds, the number of silvers and the number of bronzes. But the total is a constraint rather than a decisive criterion. Once the threshold is reached, the total number of medals ceases to apply further as a decision criterion.

Another example will help illustrate the difference between a constraint and a decisive criterion. Consider three hypothetical job offers, A, B and C. Suppose we are primarily motivated by interesting and useful work, but also have in mind a minimum salary and a maximum commute. In this situation, the salary and the time spent travelling become constraints. Let's suppose that offer A appears to be the most satisfying and would give us the shortest commute but doesn't match our salary threshold; offer B just meets both these thresholds and the project looks worthwhile; and offer C offers the best salary and a short commute but the work doesn't look very challenging. Which offer do we take? Given the way we structured the evaluation criteria, we should accept offer B. Although offer C comes with the highest salary, salary is a constraint, and therefore above the threshold ceases to be decisive, and offer A doesn't match our threshold for salary.

None of this means that we have achieved a lucid understanding of our choices. One reason why we may not be able to make a decision is because we haven't defined the criteria well enough. We may find that all the criteria we have selected are constraints and that none are decisive. This could be correct if the choice is not very important, or it could mean that there is some other aspect to the deliberation that isn't being made explicit. Similarly, it's possible that there will be multiple decisive criteria. If there are no decisive criteria or more than one, it is likely the decision-making process will be baffled. My guess is that when we find ourselves unable to make a decision, it's because we haven't distinguished decisive criteria from constraints or set the thresholds clearly enough. We don't really know what we want.

It may also be the case that the way we have set up the criteria is wrong. We can imagine going through the job evaluation process a few times and each time coming to the conclusion that we should take offer B rather than either A or C because it meets our selection criteria. But C earns a much better salary, and now, when it comes to it, we realise we are struggling to turn this down. What should we do: take offer A, offer B or offer C, or rethink our career based on this new insight? All would be valid courses of action. The purpose of the heuristic is both to uncover what it is that is really motivating us and then structuring the criteria to arrive at the decision that best implements this discovery.

There are a number of advantages of using ordering principles rather than utility optimisation as a model of practical reasoning. The first is that an idea of rational decision-making can be applied however poorly framed the decision-making process is and however little information is available. Both challenges of practical reasoning – simplification of complexity and evaluation of incommensurable options – can be approached through the application of ordering principles. Different principles can be applied during the process. Utility optimisation assumes that simplification has been achieved, and bypasses rather than resolves the issue of incommensurability.

This means that the idea of rational decision-making can be extended to poorly defined and fluid situations and to decisions made without sufficient time or information. There is a mistaken idea that practical decision-making is irrational. This is an unfortunate by-product of the challenges posed to rational choice theory by behavioural economists. From a valid concern to show that the limited definition of rationality used in utility optimisation models in economics and decision theory is misleading, and doesn't correctly describe how people actually make decisions, the mistaken conclusion is drawn that practical reasoning in real situations is irrational, thereby perpetuating rather than challenging the basic premises.

Further, practical rationality can be given a broader meaning than simply the consistency of someone's decisions with their preferences and of their preferences with each other. There is no rationality in forcing our preferences into a consistent shape if that shape doesn't reflect our actual goals and beliefs. More than likely, these will be based on sometimes conflicting and contradictory objectives, and a rational strategy in these circumstances is likely to be one that accepts these contradictions and, as it were, backs a number of horses.

Practical reasoning has caused more trouble for theorists than it should have. Many theoretical approaches tend to end up in some kind of two-stage processing, a non-rational process of simplification and framing followed by a rational process of decision-making. My view is that this is unnecessary. By looking at practical reasoning as a primarily heuristic process, with techniques adapted to the degree to which the problem can be defined and evaluated, the process can be seen as continuous from end to end. The problems of incommensurability are an extension of the problems of complexity. The heuristics we use to manage complexity can also to some extent be used to manage incommensurability, although the reverse isn't true because the heuristics we use to manage incommensurability assume the work of simplification has been done.

For much of the time practical reasoning is very similar to theoretical reasoning. Both are aspects of critical thinking grounded in the successful application of abstract conceptual models. Both theoretical reasoning and practical reasoning require forensic skills, that is, the ability to build and argue a case. But there is a difference in emphasis. Theoretical reasoning is concerned with developing conceptual models and with the identification of the nature of a system. Practical reasoning is concerned, firstly, with a lucid understanding of the particularity of the situation in which we have to act and how it might evolve, and secondly to identify how it might be possible to successfully intervene in the evolution of the situation. In practical reasoning we have to consider not just what is the case but what might be the case. And practical reasoning is also significantly constrained by time and lack of information.

## Intention, process and outcomes

Where does ethical value appear in this conceptual model of action and what role does it play? Ethical value contributes to the determination of objectives and strategies; it is sufficient to create a constraint, usually sufficient to determine an obligation, but not in itself sufficient to determine an objective or strategy. For this reason, it functions primarily as a set of constraints and secondarily as a set of selection criteria.

There is a significant asymmetry in the ethical domain between what should be done and what should not be done. There are many ethical paths and many unethical paths, but while a course of action's being unethical is usually sufficient grounds for us to reject it, its being ethical is not usually sufficient grounds for pursuing it. Other criteria must be applied to determine which among many ethical actions we will take. There is therefore a lack of symmetry between ethical prescriptions and ethical prohibitions, which means that values function primarily as constraints, and only secondarily, if at all, as selection criteria.

Knowledge, liberty, justice, peace, happiness and prosperity are background states rather than intentions, actions or outcomes. It isn't sufficient simply to desire them as a state. Just as you cannot speak 'language' but must always speak a particular language, states such as justice and peace must necessarily take some particular form. But this isn't true of their contraries: oppression, conflict, poverty, unhappiness and ignorance. This is because we don't want them to be the state in whatever form they might appear.

However, in order to think about ethical value, we need to add two further dimensions to the model. There is the process through which intentions are turned into actions and the process through which actions lead to outcomes. Ethical values can be applied to the course of action as a whole and to each of these phases. But there are always gaps between intention, action and outcome. To be successful we need to be able to bridge both the gap between intention and process and the gap between process and outcome. And because there are gaps, it is possible that the ethical value of the intention, the ethical value of the action and the ethical value of the outcome may diverge.

The gaps between intentions, actions and outcomes mean that outcomes can be influenced but not determined. We are always dealing, at best, with likely consequences. Intentions can fail to turn into appropriate actions for many reasons. The gap between what we intend to do and what we actually do can be a consequence of many factors: lack of skill, lack of attention, lack of self-control. In Ancient Greek thinking these last two were captured in the idea of *akrasia*, or weakness of the will. *Akrasia* means knowing what you want to do or what you ought to do but not being able to carry this through to the right action. Good intentions often evaporate in misconceived actions or in inaction – and so, perhaps fortunately, do many ill intentions.

And intentions can also be wrong. It may be that our intentions are the consequence of a misreading of the situation or due to faulty assumptions, information or reasoning. Intentions have to be discovered, recovered, constructed and interpreted. They may be superficial. It may turn out that the intention was a mistake, the consequence of a failure to understand what it is that we do actually want or need.

The gap between the actions we take and the outcomes that follow can also be a consequence of many factors. I don't know if there is a term to describe the reasons why actions don't always create the expected outcomes. The law of unintended consequences captures something of the idea. We may choose the wrong strategy through lack of information or failure to interpret the information we have correctly. We may lack the skill to carry out the strategy, or we may lack the forensic abilities to build our case and the bargaining skills necessary to carry other participants with us.

But even when we have a lucid understanding of ourselves and the circumstances, we can be defeated by the complexity of the situation. Fundamentally, courses of action are pursued over a shared terrain and we have only limited influence over how the other participants will respond. There isn't always a solution or a deal. It may be that there isn't a path from intention to outcome, and the desired outcome is simply out of reach.

The second dimension that must be added are the levels at which ethical values function. One set operates at the level of the transaction. The constraints here are typically constraints on strategies based on fraud, theft, violence, intimidation and exploitation; and by extension these constraints exclude objectives that can only be reached by such methods.

Ethical values primarily function at the transactional level as a set of constraints. One reason is that making ethical values into selection criteria would focus on motivations rather than actions and outcomes. A second reason is that they tend only to work as strategies if they are the exception. Fraud is a kind of miscommunication, but normally the intention behind deception is not to undermine communication as such, because the fraud only works if there is an expectation of reliable communication. A fraud exploits this expectation. Similarly, the intention of theft isn't to undermine the institution of property but to exploit the conventions of property ownership. In a society without property, it is difficult to see what theft would mean as a strategy. I think the same is true of violence, intimidation and exploitation. The benefit from these strategies comes when they are the exception to the usual conduct of society. Acting violently in a violent society might be the only way of surviving, but it would be a strategy of damage limitation rather than an attempt to create an advantage.

A second set of values operates at the level of character and motivation and is concerned with the success and failure of projects. This is the terrain of *akrasia* and human frailty. The positive values are self-control and attention. The list of human frailties is a long one: excess, greed, recklessness, negligence, inattention, self-deception, wilful ignorance, complacency, over-confidence and so on.

A third set of values operates also at the level of character and motivation but is concerned more with identity and self-image, with what type of person we want to be, rather than with the narrower questions of success and failure. I have in mind here the values of integrity and ambition, generosity and meanness, kindness and unkindness. Are our objectives and strategies worthy of us?

Something these values have in common that becomes more visible when they are categorised in this way is how far they all function to build confidence. Deception, theft, intimidation, violence and exploitation undermine our confidence in the reliability and integrity of social courses of action. Lack of self-control and inattention undermine our confidence in the reliability of the other participants, and a lack of integrity undermines our confidence in their presentation of their identity. In this way, ethical principles are abstractions that serve as repositories for the lessons learned from experience about how to build societies.

This analysis is predicated on the idea that ethical value is a component of practical reasoning, decision-making and participation in a course of action and can be best understood by modelling these activities. This makes sense to me, but much modern thinking about ethics has tended to approach the topic through the investigation of attitudes, knowledge and language. Are ethical values something you can know about in the same way that you can know about biology and economics? Do ethical terms refer to things in the same way that the words *tree* and *house* refer to things?

With a statement such as 'slavery is wrong', what is actually being said? Three models in particular have been advocated recently: the expressivist, the subjectivist and the realist. The expressivist view is that the statement is reporting the speaker's attitude. We shouldn't ask if the statement is true, but rather whether or not it was made sincerely. The subjectivist view anchors moral value in human nature and the human condition, so the statement becomes a reflection of the interests and experience of the speaker or the speaker's tribe. Naturalism tends to ethical subjectivism and subjectivism is probably the prevailing approach today. The right question here might be: does the speaker have a lucid understanding of the human predicament? The ethical realist's view, in contrast, is that value is discernible in the nature of the world, so that the question becomes: does the speaker have a lucid understanding of the cosmos?

However, what all these perspectives have in common is the idea that moral statements are existential statements. Moral statements succeed or fail in so far as they refer or fail to refer to some aspect of the actual world, whether this is the speaker's attitude, the human condition or the nature of the cosmos.

My view, on the other hand, is that moral statements are classifications. To label an action fraudulent, for example, is to classify it as belonging to the population of fraudulent actions. Like every classification, the concept of fraud is a component of a hierarchy of classifications. At a more specific levels in the hierarchy we can describe the type of fraud more precisely: untruth, misinformation, distraction, evasion, hypocrisy, counterfeit and so on. At the most abstract levels in the hierarchy we use the terms 'good' and 'bad' and 'right' and 'wrong'. These are the most abstract terms for approbation and disapprobation and extend beyond the ethical domain, so that we can speak about a good intention, a good solution, a good article, a good tool, a good performance, a good painting; the right intention, the right solution, the right tool and so on. Because these terms are so abstract, there is little commonality and it isn't possible to understand the meaning without more information. Good and bad and right and wrong can be, among other things, assessments of form, functioning, workmanship, fit and execution, and typically there will be a shared idea about what these terms mean in each context.

A model for the grammar here might be the way we use the term *item*. An item can be anything: an item on an agenda, an item of news, an item in the accounts, an item of inventory, an item of clothing, an item in a shopping basket. These things don't have or need to have any attributes in common. The common idea is that there is a collection of objects and an item is one object in the collection. Not all parts of wholes are items; there is a looseness about how an item belongs to a collection. It's a low specification term for objects that are part of some sort of collection, and as it is fairly common it's convenient to have a term for this situation. It certainly seems possible to contrive an idea about goodness and badness, but I am not sure it's really any more useful than trying to find the nature or essence of item-hood.

Good and bad and right and wrong are very convenient summary or shorthand terms, but they are always summaries or shorthand for less abstract, more substantive terms. 'Slavery is wrong' is a summary, shorthand way of saying something like this: the intentions, actions and outcomes that compose the institution of slavery are a subset of the total population of wrongful intentions, actions and outcomes, and what puts them in this category is that the institution of slavery is not possible without strategies of fraud, theft, violence, intimidation and exploitation, and a disregard for the dignity and autonomy of human beings.

The difference between existential statements and classifications is that while existential statements can be true or false at a very granular level, classificatory frameworks have a domain of application as a structure. The link between them is that classificatory frameworks are applied through existential statements and it is the scope, simplicity and applicability with which existential statements can be made that serves to define the domain of application of the classificatory structure and whether that structure is a success or not. Every existential statement is like a tether that binds the classification to its domain of application. This implies that moral arguments are real arguments that can be settled objectively.

From this perspective, the criterion for the success of an ethical model overlaps with the success criteria for a scientific theory, although there are a number of significant differences between ethical models and scientific models. Firstly, the domain of applicability of an ethical model extends beyond the actual world to the world as it can be imagined, whereas a scientific model that doesn't apply to the actual universe would have little value. Secondly, because outcomes cannot be contrived, ethical theories cannot be tested in the same way that scientific theories can be tested by success in predicting the outcome of a process. Ethical models can't be used to make predictions. Thirdly, because we undertake ethical arguments as participants rather than as observers, we are engaged in them in a way that we aren't with scientific reasoning.

But what ethical theories and scientific theories have in common is that both should accurately describe a large class of observations on the basis of a model that contains only a few arbitrary elements.

## The problem of means and ends

Why do we waste our time doing things we don't value? Some of the time this is because the task is imposed on us, some of the time because the task has become routine and habitual, some of the time because we have to react to the course of events. But on other occasions we undertake tasks as a means to an end; we do something we don't value in order to achieve something we do. In his theory of social action, Max Weber called the thinking that supports these courses of action *'Zweckrationalität'*, or goal-oriented reasoning.

Goal-oriented reasoning is instrumental reasoning. A means to an end is a course of action pursued in order to change the current state of affairs into a desirable future state, and instrumental reasoning is thinking about how this can best be achieved. Goal-oriented reasoning is concerned with success, with problem solving and with the application of technology. As a consequence, the value of an action identified as a means is contingent on the circumstances, and its pursuit is dependent on the situation and context.

The alternative is a course of action pursued for its own sake as an end in itself. Such a course of action is performed without consideration for its outcome or the possibility of success. The value comes from the performance. The value of an action identified as an end is therefore independent of the situation and the context. The thinking that underlies such courses of action Weber called *'Wertrationalität'*, or value-oriented reasoning.

Value-oriented reasoning is concerned with the rationality, legitimacy and the authenticity of a course of action rather than its outcome. Weber suggested that values have their source in religion, ethics and art.

The difference between goal-oriented and value-oriented reasoning is that, whereas instrumental reasoning seeks to identify how to turn the current state into a desirable future state, value-oriented reasoning is concerned with the closeness to type of a course of action. There is no time dimension to value-oriented reasoning. The question of rationality is how close the attributes of this course of action are to the attributes of a rational course of action, the question of legitimacy is how close they are to the attributes of a legitimate course of action, and the question of authenticity is how close they are to the attributes of an authentic course of action.

It is possible within the model that a course of action may be pursued both as a means to an end and as an end in itself, but the implication is that, in so far as it is a means, we think instrumentally, and in so far as it is an end, we think in terms of value. However, I think there remains a problem with this analysis, a problem that is a consequence of linking the motivation for a course of action to the type of reasoning engaged in.

Practical reasoning requires both goal-oriented reasoning and value-oriented reasoning. What we think of as a means to an end is an action in a situation where every other value has been stripped away. It is obvious because it is isolated, like a rock revealed at low tide. But by itself, instrumental reasoning gives no direction and, similarly, value-oriented reasoning without instrumental reasoning is just a diagnosis; a theoretical analysis of a situation.

This suggests some adjustments to Weber's model. Rationality, including both instrumental rationality and value-oriented rationality, is, like legitimacy and authenticity, a constraining value on a course of action. Ideally, imagined as a Venn diagram, the course we take will fall within the intersection of all three, but this isn't always possible, and we may have to compromise, choosing one or two out of the three – legitimacy and authenticity instead of rationality, for example. On the other hand, in very adverse circumstances, where there are no good choices, we might support a course that has the merit of being rational simply because it is rational, even if we don't care about the outcome, because our motivation is to sustain, in so far as it is possible, a rational world. Rationality, like legitimacy and authenticity, rather than being the driver for actions that we don't value, might provide some redemption for tasks that we cannot avoid. A chore is a chore, but if it is, at least in its own terms, rational, it may be possible to accept the burden more gracefully.

From an abstract perspective, instrumental reasoning is a process of mapping the current state of the system to a future state of the system based on a knowledge of how the system components behave, how the system is therefore likely to evolve, and how it might be possible to intervene to achieve a particular outcome.

That the intervention is instrumentally rational is also therefore a constraint on what interventions can be made.

Instrumental reasoning requires a process of discovery and invention that may fail. For example, bureaucratic processes often become self-sustaining, so that what starts out as the process supporting a strategy becomes detached from its original purpose and becomes a procedure without a purpose. We could say that the means has become the end, but this wouldn't be psychologically true. The routine and banal contains the ever-present danger that what began as purpose-oriented action has become detached from its original rationale and no longer has any purpose other than its own repetition.

Although there is no time dimension to value-oriented reasoning, the value of time is woven into instrumental rationality and therefore into practical reasoning. By its nature a strategy takes time to unfold. A strategy that takes too long to play out will create a problem because there is a balance to be found between present and future. Value can be wholly deferred or wholly realised now, but more usually the objective is to distribute the realisation of value through time.

The project model can illustrate this. A strategy is designed to direct a set of resources towards the attainment of a set of objectives within a set of constraints. From this perspective, objectives and constraints determine strategies, and from this is it might appear that strategic thinking is goal-oriented and thinking about objectives and constraints is value-oriented.

But project planning is rarely a simple linear process. The structure of a project as a whole has to be flexible enough to accommodate and adjust to the course of events. Objectives must be modified when there is no path to achieving them, and constraints can be relaxed if they block all the paths to the objective. Perhaps the original plan turns out to be too expensive, so we adjust the objectives to make it more affordable. Perhaps we started out with the intention to avoid borrowing money to fund the project, but as the costs rise, we find we have to remove this constraint.

Strategies are created to achieve objectives within constraints, but in the process of deliberation and negotiation each component of the structure can be modified. Objectives and constraints cannot be entirely fixed, and strategies cannot be entirely disposable. They must all engage in a dance in order to achieve a perhaps-only-temporary harmony.

Strategies are developed in the context of the resources that are to hand and the contingencies of the situation. A strategy that is too rigid and that can't be adapted to changes in the situation is likely to fail. However, the value of strategy comes from the constraints it imposes. If the strategy changes in response to every change in the situation, it will provide no structure or guidance towards decision-making. This is the reason strategies are usually organised into hierarchies: to allow as much small-scale tactical flexibility as possible within a broader-scale strategic stability.

A way to think about this is to think in terms of degree of substitutability. At one end of the scale we have objectives, strategies and constraints to which we have little attachment. These are the fungible components. At the other end of the scale we have objectives, strategies and constraints to which we are deeply attached. These are the actions and outcomes that we are unwilling to give up; they are, non-negotiable. Overlaying these assessments, and sometimes in tension with them, are the formal and structural requirements of each component of the project. If we make this adjustment, we can take a more holistic view of a project. Instead of fixed ends and disposable means, each component of the structure is to a greater or lesser extent substitutable. Furthermore, what applies to the components also applies to the project as a whole, which is also to a greater or lesser degree substitutable.

Rather than being a linear and sequential process of instrumental reasoning, the processes of deliberation and negotiation are heuristic. Practical reasoning isn't primarily puzzle solving. Objectives, strategies and constraints are adjusted to adapt to and accommodate each other and to the situation until an equilibrium of some kind is achieved. It is a process of both discovery and invention: discovering what we actually value, and inventing paths to achieve it.

Another way of describing this limitation is that the means and ends model doesn't have an obvious place for constraints. Strategies map to means and objectives map to ends, but both strategies and objectives are subject to constraints. My argument is that the constraints are both the primary form-giving component of a course of action and the principal vehicle for the expression of values. The constraints are the banks within which the river flows. The constraints of rationality, legitimacy and authenticity apply both to the project as a whole and to the specific objectives and strategies designed to achieve it.

Not every course of action is sufficiently well-ordered to be thought of as a project. A course of action doesn't have to have an objective, and there therefore doesn't have to be a strategy. A course of action may be routine, banal, wayward and reactive. The absence of strategy implies either actions that are routine and habitual or merely tactical. The only constant is that there are always constraints determined by a set of values and by the course of events. There is always a background, even when there is no foreground.

The nature of practical reasoning is shown in the story Sartre tells, in *Existentialism is a Humanism*, about a student who came to him for advice during the Second World War. The student's father, inclined towards collaboration, was in conflict with his mother. His brother had been killed in the German offensive of 1940. He wanted revenge for his brother's death, but his mother now lived alone with him, and finds with him her only consolation in life. His choice was therefore to abandon his mother to fight with the Free French forces, or to remain with her. He knew his departure and the possibility of his death would plunge his mother into despair. He also knew that every action he took to support her directly aided her, whereas every action to depart and fight was an ambiguous act that might serve no purpose and could be lost in the sands. He might, for instance, have found himself filing forms somewhere in England. He therefore found himself faced with two types of action, one concrete and immediate, but addressed to only one person, and the other indeterminate and uncertain, but addressed to the fate of the whole nation. And he was faced with two types of morality: on the one hand, a morality of sympathy and personal devotion; and on the other a morality of public service, of service to state and people.

Already in this case the value of time and the distribution of probabilities have been thought through and no decision has become clear. Both courses of action are rational and both courses of action are legitimate. This is a process of reasoning and may be wrong. Perhaps the instrumental reasoning is wrong and the assessment of the outcome in each case is mistaken. Perhaps the sense of legitimacy is wrong. A traditionalist might suggest that an ethic of public service is more appropriate for a man, and an ethic of private devotion for a woman.

In this case, therefore, the student is faced with the question of authenticity. But authenticity is not obvious. Sartre argues that you have to choose, because there is nowhere to look for the answer. Even self-knowledge will not tell you, because you won't know who you are until you make the choice. In this case, what is left at the end of this process of deliberation is the idea that the authentic decision is the one that you can assume responsibility for.

## Moral reasoning

If practical reasoning is a process of deliberation and negotiation that comes to a conclusion in a decision – or sometimes in the lack of a decision – then moral reasoning is reasoning about what values are to be applied in the process of practical reasoning and how this is to be done. As a component of decision-making, it is concerned with two questions: what set of values should guide the selection of objectives and strategies, and what set of values should constrain them. However, moral reasoning extends beyond decision-making to cover judgements and justifications, mitigations, accusations and excuses. It is not just a question of making our own decisions, but also our making judgements regarding how everybody else is reaching their decisions.

The reasoning behind a judgement is different from the reasoning behind a decision. Timing makes a difference. Justifications can look quite different before and after the event. After the event, the outcome is known, whereas before only possibilities and probabilities could be considered, and the actual outcome may not have been foreseen at all. If things went well it becomes possible to defend an action retrospectively by looking at the outcome. If things didn't go as hoped, it may be that the intention and the process are sufficient to mitigate the blame, even though the strategy didn't succeed. Judgements also have a different focus, primarily concerned with the legitimacy of a course of action, rather than the rationality and authenticity that are also important to the person making the decision.

Mitigations are often conflated with justifications, but the two things are different. Mitigations are very important in moral arguments because they provide a balance to the requirement for justification. Decisions are often hurried and made with incomplete information. Mistakes get made. Things go wrong. Mitigations look at the gaps between intention, process and outcome. If the intentions were good and the process was well thought out, this can be put towards mitigating blame for unhappy outcomes. Conversely, when motives are suspect and the process careless, a fortunate outcome might mitigate these shortcomings. Mitigations are a form of excuse, but whereas excuses tend to be exercises in evasion and distraction, mitigations are necessary to any workable system of accountability. Another aspect of the distinction is to say that you can claim a justification, but only appeal to a mitigation.

There is also the question of the spirit in which moral reasoning is undertaken. Moral reasoning is often a search for permission rather than a search for guidance, the unvoiced question being *what can I get away*? Casuistry, the application of ethical principles to particular situations, has acquired a negative connotation precisely for this reason. In this respect, Kierkegaard's is the most instructive approach. In his argument, the choice is not between interpretations of the ethical life, but only whether to engage in the ethical life at all. This isn't a question of adhering to or applying one or another set of principles and ideas, but rather adopting an attitude that embraces the serious examination and application of ethical values.

If the two basic challenges of practical reasoning are simplification and incommensurability, ethical values play an ambivalent role in simplifying practical reasoning and function as a complicating factor in the face of incommensurability. Because ethical constraints rule out of consideration many objectives and strategies, they function much of the time to simplify decision-making. However, ethical values are incommensurable and can conflict, and when this happens judgements become more difficult. And it can happen that there is no ethically acceptable path available, which turns a problem into a test of character rather than one of reasoning.

There is little structure for prioritisation or conflict resolution between values. Because of the asymmetry between ethical values and their negation, there is always an inherent ordering: justice, truth and generosity rather than injustice, deceit and meanness. But what happens when truth conflicts with peace or knowledge with happiness? Autonomy is an awkward value, and so is justice. In principle claims might be expected to take priority over appeals, but, even though the demand for justice is the most compelling ethical claim that can be made, delivering justice is sometimes inconvenient, and appeals to the values of compassion, forgiveness and mercy, and the necessities of peace, rescue and reconciliation can all function in one way or another to limit or compromise a just outcome.

Normative ethical theories typically seek to find a framework within which these kinds of difficulties can be addressed. Is there a way of prioritising some values over others? How far can ethical values be adapted to circumstances? Should we be concerned primarily with intentions, with process or with outcomes? Should our ethical thinking be fundamentally inward looking and concerned with motivation and character, or should it be fundamentally outward looking and concerned with process and outcomes?

The rules of the road and the rules for the conduct of meetings are examples of normative frameworks. They describe how things should happen in a way that guides participants to actually make them happen. In the same way, a normative ethical theory would offer guidance to someone faced with a conflict like the one between justice and compassion. It might advise a judge to 'focus on the defendant's intentions' in cases of doubt or perhaps to 'prioritise compassion when the correctional system is unreliable'.

One approach to thinking about this question is by taking the negative way. It is sometimes easier to say what something is not than what it is. What, for example, does it mean for moral reasoning to be irrecoverably misconceived? For a Platonist, it would be a line of argument undertaken in ignorance of reality, where reality is in the domain of Ideas. For an Aristotelian it would be a judgement not grounded in an understanding of what human excellence looks like. For a natural law theorist such as Thomas Aquinas it would be a course of action that was out of harmony with the providential plan that orders the cosmos.

These ideas have a long tradition, but similar exclusions can be identified in more recent ways of thinking. Here are three examples, but this isn't an exhaustive list. The first stems from the modern commitment to universalism based on egalitarian and individualist assumptions. These assumptions exclude appeals to natural hierarchies, to essentialist understandings of gender, ethnicity or nation, and to arguments that posit a model of society as a functionally modular structure where different classes have different roles and therefore different permissions and obligations. Because these assumptions are the building blocks of traditional ways of thinking about human society, the shift to a modern framework in a society almost always leads to conflict.

That said, however, appeals to universality are necessary but not sufficient. For example, the Kantian categorical imperative rules out lying in any circumstance and whatever the consequences. By its nature a categorical imperative must therefore trump a hypothetical imperative. The problem with Kantian ethics is that the distinction between a categorical and a hypothetical imperative contains no calibration for importance or significance. It is a formal requirement based on the possibility of universality. If, as can often happen, the ethics of personal integrity governed by a categorical imperative come into conflict with the ethics of public service governed by a hypothetical imperative, we might quite reasonably want the hypothetical imperative to prevail.

A second approach flows from the metaphysics of philosophical naturalism. In this context naturalism is the idea that moral values are attributes of human culture and society in the same way that the scientific facts are attributes of nature and can therefore be studied by similar methods to those used in the natural sciences.

Arguments within this framework seek to ground moral value in psychological naturalism in the manner of utilitarianism or to link them to an interpretation of evolutionary biology.

To this way of thinking, moral arguments that draw on the metaphysics of religion or that posit magical agents and powers are misconceived. However, this also creates a fundamental problem for naturalism, because it assumes that ethics is continuous with nature and cannot recognise that there is also a discontinuity. It not only excludes the religious and the magical, but also the introspective self, the platform on which ethical life is built. This is an unsolvable structural problem, because this exclusion is a facet of the external point of view that flows from the move to exclude the subject of cognizance from natural science.

A third possibility is arguments derived from the concept of natural and human rights. The model of rights, discretions and obligations is an elegant one. Rights and discretions go together in the way that the two sides of a piece of paper go together; a right claimed by one person implies a matching absence of discretion on the part of everyone else, and a discretion claimed by one person implies an absence of rights on the part of others. The absence of discretion carries with it an implied duty of care, otherwise discretion could be exercised through negligence and inattention.

The right to self-defence can be thought of as a limitation on the duty of care. The right to life is the idea that our lives are not lived at the discretion of anyone else. We have, at the same time, an absence of discretion and a duty of care with regard to the lives of others. But while the absence of discretion is unlimited, the duty of care has boundaries. We cannot acquire discretion over the life of another, even a violent assailant, but such an assailant isn't protected by the same duty of care.

Whether or not a right exists is an objective judgement. For example, a prisoner suffers a loss of freedom but retains a right to medical treatment. The right exists because there is both an absence of discretion on the part of the prison authorities and a corresponding duty of care. The prison governor can neither make a discretionary choice nor avoid summoning medical help for a sick prisoner. Such a right is a legislated one, and law-makers could decide otherwise, but I have never heard of any doing so. The reason is that doing so would be vindictive in motivation and thereby undermine the legitimacy of the justice system.

The model of natural and human rights isn't grounded in something more fundamental. It's a system of interlocking concepts. If we keep pressing and ask why there can be a right, can we give an answer? I would argue that the concept of rights is grounded in opposition to the concept of sovereignty. It's a model that excludes appeals to the arbitrary. The idea of natural rights was originally developed in the 17th century in response to claims by sovereigns that they had discretion over every aspect of the lives of their subjects, including whether they might live or not. But the model also excludes appeals to sovereignty that are based on other grounds, such as the nation or the people.

Moral reasoning can appear to be overwhelmingly complex. The advantage of this kind of analysis is that it allows some high-level organisation and supports some focusing. It implies that moral reasoning takes place at different levels. From my own perspective, for example, a line of reasoning grounded in the framework of philosophical naturalism will not work any better than a line of reasoning grounded in the idea of natural law or Platonic realism. Similarly, appeals to hierarchy and functional role or to sovereignty and arbitrary power will fail.

This doesn't mean that these ideas are wrong *a priori* or offer no insight, nor does it mean that appeals to universality or to non-arbitrary principles will succeed. These appeals are necessary but not sufficient. The purpose of this analysis is to understand what is at stake and locate where the divergence of opinion occurs, not to settle the disagreement.

We are still some distance from concrete decision-making. A more focused model that is of value in this context distinguishes what might be called an *ethics of conviction* from an *ethics of responsibility*. These are the usual translations of the terms *Gesinnungsethik* and *Verantwortungsethik*, given currency by Max Weber in his essay *Politics as a Vocation*. *Gesinnung* means 'cast of mind' or 'attitude', and *Verantwortung* means 'answerability', 'responsibility' or 'accountability'. Weber argued that politics particularly requires an ethic of responsibility because politics is a conflict over the use of administrative coercion. Sometimes unjust and harmful actions are required in the pursuit of a wider good or the avoidance of a wider harm. Politicians must sometimes make hard choices that put the public good ahead of particular justice. *Fiat justitia, et pereat mundus* - let justice be done though the world perish - is a stirring motto, but potentially dangerous and damaging in the real world.

However, the distinction applies in every domain of moral reasoning and the outcome is often less clear than it is in politics. An ethics of responsibility tends to focus attention outward to the situation and the outcome, the participants taking responsibility not just for the intended outcome but for all consequences of their actions. An ethics of conviction focuses attention inward, on the intentions and character of the actors. The basic critique of an ethics of conviction is that it is self-serving, more concerned with the state of the actor's soul than harm and suffering in the world, and it might appear that the advantage lies with an ethics of responsibility.

However, the basic justification for such an ethics of conviction is that outcomes cannot be contrived. Events may be influenced but they cannot be determined. The terrain has to be navigated. Outcomes are the products of negotiation, and negotiation is a process that inherently requires compromises. There has to be bargaining and negotiation between the parties involved, and in such a negotiation the parties must respect the integrity and the separateness of other parties. An ethics of responsibility goes astray when it leads to the appropriation of the responsibilities proper to others. An ethics of conviction respects the autonomy of others because it limits the answerability of the agent for the contingency of outcomes, while an ethics of responsibility places unlimited demands on an agent, which inevitably reduces the status of the other participants from equals to instruments.

The argument between the ethics of conviction and the ethics of responsibility is a real one. Conflicts are inevitable because there are gaps between intention, process and outcome that cannot be bridged. There are therefore shearing layers in ethical thinking, unresolvable strains in the system.

There is an ethic of conviction and an ethic of responsibility in both religious and secular thinking. Because religious thinking posits a providential or karmic cosmos, there will always be the danger of impiety, of overstepping, in anyone taking too much responsibility for outcomes. On the other hand, a reliance on providence or karma can lead to recklessness or indifference from a sense that the consequences of our actions are being looked after elsewhere.

The balance looks different from the secular perspective. There is nothing to offend against in an indifferent universe, but equally there is nothing else to take responsibility. Secularism can also lead in opposite directions: one direction leads towards frivolousness and irresponsibility, the other towards an improper assumption of all the burdens of the world.

Moral reasoning tends to give out when there are no good paths. It also gives out when there is more than one good path. Sartre's story of the student faced with a choice between an ethic of personal devotion and an ethic of public service illustrates the difficulty. The first part of the process is to determine what the situation is, which might be called the requirement for lucidity. The student has a clear view of the situation, though there remains the possibility that he is mistaken. The second part of the process is to determine questions of legitimacy, whether there are prior commitments and obligations. In this case there are no specific commitments but two non-specific commitments: a duty to the public good and a duty to family.

The third part of the reasoning process might be to ask: what will be authentic for me, what course of action am I willing to be accountable for? Sartre's own purpose in telling the story is to argue that we cannot know what is authentic until we have made the choice; you cannot know you are the sort of person who will lend money to a friend until you have lent money to a friend. You cannot know if you are the kind of person who chooses service in the army over care for your mother until you have made that choice.

I am not sure this is entirely right; perhaps it is true for a student with little personal history to draw on. Value-oriented reasoning depends on processes of discovery and invention, and therefore takes time and experience to acquire. And if you have, thus far, followed one ethical path, for example by putting public service first, the question becomes a slightly different one. You do to some extent know what sort of person you are, but a hesitation implies that maybe you are not quite sure whether that has been the right person, or will still be the right person in the future.

## What are we arguing about?

What exactly is at issue in an ethical conflict? Is it a question of facts and their interpretation? Or is it that different values are being applied? Or are ethical disagreements proxies for something else?

Certainly, lack of candour is ubiquitous in ethical disagreements. The justifications we offer to others are not always the same as the justifications we give to ourselves. Reasons offered as justifications turn out to be rationalisations and pretexts. Mitigations are put forward as justifications. Arguments are aired to send signals rather than to carry information, signals that are designed to rally and encourage supporters and daunt potential opponents. They may be political advocacy, disguises for a conflict of interest, or be part of a rhetorical strategy. Or, more simply, lack of candour may be a sign of a lack of clarity and self-knowledge, or even just clumsiness and lack of skill.

Such arguments are difficult to deal with. Timing counts, and a rationalisation or pretext will have succeeded if unravelling it takes up time and energy and the moment when it matters is passed. And there are complexities. Evasion and distraction can look very like tact and courtesy, and it may be that what is tactful with regard to one person is at the same time evasive with regard to someone else with no way out of the conflict. There is perhaps a kind of necessary hypocrisy that is also a necessary tact. And honest communication requires an honest audience as much as honest speakers.

It is also certainly true that disagreement reflects differences in values. There will always be an authentic conflict of values. The value we place on the passing of time and the balance between the long view and the short view is a personal one. So are our attitudes to uncertainty and to risk.

However, most if not all contentious ethical issues also reflect fault-lines in the way we understand the world to be and our interpretation of events. Moral argument intersects with knowledge, experience and imagination. World views are at least in principle about the objective world, they are not reports about our feelings or our interests and preferences. Even within a single ethical framework, it is always difficult to work out how the general principles apply to particular cases. When the argument is across different frames of reference and varying metaphysical assumptions, it becomes very difficult to make any kind of progress.

My own view is that there is much less genuine moral disagreement than might be supposed by the intractability of moral arguments. Our moral understanding has multiple layers, some of which are personal and subjective but most of which reflect our understanding of the nature of the world we inhabit.

One example of a fundamental fault-line is the one between the modern industrial and traditional agrarian models of society. Traditional agrarian models typically function in terms of natural hierarchies and the idea that everyone has a station-in-life within these hierarchies, a station determined by combinations of caste and class and gender and age, which in turn governs occupation, behaviour and obligations. Each person belongs to a class and different functions are attributed to each class, such that each makes a different contribution to the operation of society as a whole. Traditional authority has to rest somewhere; maybe in the past or on what has always been done or as a part of the cosmic order. To a traditional way of thinking, differences in status and role are woven into the fabric of nature.

When modern values conflict with traditional values there cannot be a meeting of minds. The traditionalist thinks the modern is a poor traditionalist and the modern thinks the traditionalist is a poor modern.

The 'official' version of modernity in Western thinking is built on ideas about equality and individualism. These two assumptions carry most of the load. The assumption of equality is more precisely the absence of natural hierarchies, and the assumption of individualism is more precisely the absence of imposed stations and roles in life. This makes every individual a principal. From this follows a requirement for the universality of ethics and the justification for personal autonomy and the dignity of the individual. It is also the basic premise of representative democracy.

This argument can be illustrated more specifically by thinking about the institution of slavery. Why is slavery morally wrong, so wrong that what could once be regarded as a natural state of affairs is now seen as a crime against humanity? I think the answer is because the offence isn't only one of aggression, intimidation, violence, fraud, theft and exploitation, but because it seeks to change a person's classification from principal to property or equipment. It is a denial of and therefore a threat to the modern ideal of humanity.

But this hasn't always been the case, and slavery was being defended by respectable opinion until relatively recently. If the moral wrongness of slavery is a question of facts and interpretations, then the mistake being made should also be one of facts and interpretations. And this kind of change can be detected. For example, Kant, writing towards the end of the 18th century, seems to have shifted his position. His earlier works reflected contemporary physiology and the idea that there was a hierarchy of human races, a hierarchy that accorded a privileged position to Europeans. He therefore adopted ideas that were, at best, ambivalent about the spread of European civilisation and the exploitation that accompanied it. In his later writing, he came to the view that physiology is not relevant to what it means to live as a human being, and therefore he was able to be much less equivocal in describing and criticising the aggressions and violations of European colonisation.

The campaign against the institution of slavery as a legal possibility was won. Slavery becomes illegal, though unfortunately it hasn't disappeared, because the facts and interpretations on which it is based become untenable. However, it didn't happen straightforwardly. There wasn't a switch that could be pressed. While slavery was legal, abolitionists were arguing not only against rival pictures of what it means to be human and the economic interests of the slave-owners but also against all the compromises, evasions and distractions inherent in the moral life.

The logic of equality is relentless. For example, marriage and parenthood were once closely linked in the structure of the family. This view requires a distinction to be drawn between legitimate and illegitimate children. But the logic of equality is that all children are equal, irrespective of the circumstances of their birth, and in the process of modernisation this equality gets written into the laws and, as a consequence, parenthood gets separated from marriage. But if marriage is no longer the grounding for parenthood, is there a reason to regard marriage as necessarily a union of a man and a woman? Prohibitions on same sex marriages start to look like arbitrary discrimination and the logic of equality insists that all unions should be treated equally. And because marriage has been separated from parenthood, there is also no fundamental reason to discriminate in the matter of adoption or other routes to parenthood.

The idea of individualism is often misunderstood. In the traditional model society tends to be seen as a functional whole. The components are classes of people each with its proper role in the operation of the whole. Individuals don't need to choose their path in life because this is already largely determined by their station-in-life. An individual who doesn't accept their role and abide by these requirements will be taken to be disrupting and damaging the functioning of society. Individualism is interpreted as self-serving and anti-social. In the modern view of society there are no stations-in-life, and therefore no defined roles, and therefore nothing to disrupt. Each individual must choose their path in life because no paths are defined or imposed. Individualism becomes the recognition of an unavoidable predicament.

Modernity is uncomfortable. Equality and individualism are based on absences, and this is probably the defining characteristic of modernity. Secularism can also be thought of as defining an absence, the absence of any sense that human destiny matters to the cosmos. This is why Sartre's existentialism, a critique of traditional ways of thinking in the context of a traditional essentialist metaphysics, cannot escape the orientation towards abandonment, anxiety and despair that comes from an awareness of and discomfort with what is absent.

The implication of this is that the content of much moral argument can therefore be right or wrong, and therefore ethical disagreements are resolvable in principle even though this is often impossible in practice. So what makes these arguments so intractable?

One reason is that the fault-lines in ethical disputes reflect load-bearing philosophical differences that aren't readily susceptible to critical thinking and forensic examination. A second is that the stakes can be very high: it may be that everything we have thought and done is in question. We cannot simply change our moral positions when we see that they can no longer be defended. The reason I think goes back to the use of heuristics and habituation. Practical reasoning is much too complicated and much too indeterminate simply to re-engineer. It is an evolved system that can only change slowly. And there is the problem of negotiating the change publicly. Something will have to be done about all our previous attitudes and stances. Too many commitments will have been made and our friends and allies may not be ready to move at the same time that we are.

This is the character of moral argument. We typically bail out of such conversations well before we reach the basic premises, or start tactful diversions, not just to protect ourselves but to protect others. We often fail to pursue these arguments to a conclusion in order to avoid the courses of action that they would commit us to. We avoid fundamental moral arguments, not because the questions cannot be resolved, but because we fear that they can.

# CHAPTER SIX

# CONCLUSION: SPRINGING THE OBJECT METHOD TRAP

In the scientific revolution of the 17th century the understanding of natural structures and the understanding of meaningful structures came apart. This separation is reflected everywhere, but is often encapsulated in the idea of the conflict between fact and value.

When I started writing this essay I made the same assumption, but in the course of putting it together I have changed my mind. I think now that facts and values have fundamentally the same function; they are both sets of constraints on the evolution of a system. Facts are constraints that function without the intermediation of intelligence, while values are constraints that function through the intermediation of intelligent minds.

For this to be the case, it must be possible for meaningful action to become the driver behind the evolution of a natural system. It must be possible for nature to become what I have been calling form-holding rather than form-giving, and the evolution of the physical universe must constrain but not determine the evolution of the meaningful cosmos. The advantage of a form-holding model is that it allows physical structures and meaningful structures to be the same. We don't need to posit any kind of dualism. Because the micro-scale is a constraint rather than a determinant, the possibility that meaningful structures at the macro-scale govern the evolution of physical systems ceases to be implausible.

In the form-holding model, the possibility of intelligence is grounded in biological stability, biological stability is grounded in chemical stability and chemical stability becomes possible when the disorder of the micro-scale world of sub-atomic particles is neutralised. In this model, the micro-scale provides the platform for the macro-scale but doesn't determine it.

This idea is neither materialist nor idealist. Nature isn't given shape by ideas until intelligent beings with access to conceptual space evolve. Structures evolve in nature with sufficient scale, stability and complexity to support intelligent beings. Intelligent beings gain access to the maps of conceptual space and can explore the abstract terrain these map makes visible and then re-build parts of nature according to this knowledge.

But these maps are independent of both nature and the human mind. By this I mean that while science bends itself to the shape of the world, the mathematics in which it is expressed does not. A differently shaped nature would generate a differently shaped science, but would use the same mathematics. Similarly, the content of our conceptual models might be different if they were being applied to a different world, but the structure of the models and the processes of abstraction and analogy through which they are created would remain the same.

Events at each scale function as constraints on events at every other scale. In a multi-layered world, a system of intersecting systems, each layer must function as a constraint on the other layers. Every system will be constrained to adapt to and accommodate every other system. If the world is metaphysically multi-layered then the method of enquiry must be constraints-oriented because the model of the cosmos as a multi-layered system of intersecting systems can only be understood through a multi-layered model of explanation, and multi-layered explanations must be constraints-oriented. A method that assumes that there are single-layered explanations on the model of the pattern of succession of cause and effect will not be able to see the world this way.

A constraints-oriented approach must be content with constrained and limited explanations rather than reaching after unequivocal and complete explanations. This way of thinking isn't going to provide the unequivocal knowledge of the kind that lies behind the assumption of the principle of sufficient reason and the idea that there are natural laws to be discovered that govern the universe. But it is I think closer to the actual practice of science. My view is that the actual practice of modern science is misunderstood and we have a false understanding of what the scientific picture is actually telling us. We don't need a new science, we just need to see the science we have more clearly. Modern science is improvised, heuristic, equivocal, incoherent and incomplete.

Constraints-oriented thinking has the advantage that it doesn't run aground on the method object problem. A multi-layered explanation isn't possible at all if explanations have to be single-layered, but a single-layered explanation is a special case of a multi-layered explanation. With a constraints-oriented model of explanation, the assumptions don't determine the conclusions.

If the world is a system of intersecting systems, a constraints-oriented method will support that discovery. If it turns out that the world can be given a single-layered explanation, it will support that as a discovery also. The goal should be to create a conceptual model such that whatever the truth is, we will be able to see it and be confident that it isn't just an artefact of the way we think but a genuine discovery about the way the world works.

REFERENCE

# LIST OF SOURCES

Andersen, H., Barker, P., & Chen, X. (1996). Kuhn's mature philosophy of science and cognitive psychology. *Philosophical Psychology, Vol. 9*(No. 3).

Brand, S. (1994). *How Buildings Learn*. New York: Viking Press.

Cilliers, P. (1998). *Complexity & Postmodernism*. London: Routledge.

Damasio, A. (2018). *The Strange Order of Things*. New York: Pantheon Books.

Dennett, D. (2013). *Intuition Pumps and Other Tools for Thinking*. New York: W.W. Norton & Company.

Dreyfus, H. L. (2008). Why Heideggerian AI Failed and how fixing it would require making it more Heideggerian. In P. Husbands, O. Holland, & M. Wheeler, *The Mechanical Mind in History*. Cambridge, Mass: MIT Press.

Dyson, F. (2002, March 28). Science & Religion: No Ends in Sight. *New York Review of Books, 49*(5). Retrieved from New York Review of Books: http://www.nybooks.com/articles/2002/03/28/science-religion-no-ends-in-sight/

Feynman, R. (1963). *Lectures on Physics*. Retrieved from California Institute of Technology: http://www.feynmanlectures.caltech.edu/

Fodor, J. (2007, May 24). Headaches Have Themselves. *London Review of Books, 29*(10), pp. 9-10. Retrieved from http://www.lrb.co.uk/v29/n10/jerry-fodor/headaches-have-themselves

Godfrey-Smith, P. (2003). *Theory and Reality*. Chicago: University of Chicago Press.

Godfrey-Smith, P. (2013, January 24). Not Sufficiently Reassuring. *London Review of Books, 35*(2), pp. 20-21. Retrieved from https://www.lrb.co.uk/v35/n02/peter-godfrey-smith/not-sufficiently-reassuring

Godfrey-Smith, P. (2017). *Other Minds*. London: William Collins.

Goodwin, B. (1997). *How the Leopard Changed its Spots*. London: Phoenix.

Hawking, S. (1988). *A Brief History of Time*. London: Transworld Publishers Ltd.

Heidegger, M. (1947). The Letter on Humanism. In *Pathmarks*. Cambridge: Cambridge University Press.

Hitchcock, C. (n.d.). *Probabilistic Causation*. (E. N. Zalta, Ed.) Retrieved from The Stanford Encyclopedia of Philosophy: https://plato.stanford.edu/archives/win2016/entries/causation-probabilistic

Jaynes, J. (n.d.). (M. Kuijsten, Editor) Retrieved from Julian Jaynes Society: www.julianjaynes.org

Kahneman, D. (2011). *Thinking, Fast and Slow*. 2011: Penguin.

Kierkegaard, S. (1843). Either/Or: A Fragment of Life. In R. Bretall, *A Kiergegaard Anthology* (pp. 19-108). Princeton: Princeton University Press.

Kripke, S. (1980). *Naming and Necessity*. Oxford: Basil Blackwell.

Maynard Smith, J. (1998). *Shaping Life*. London: Weidenfeld & Nicholson.

Nagel, T. (2012). *Mind & Cosmos*. Oxford: Oxford University Press.

Powell, C. S. (2015, October 29). Will Quantum Mechanics Swallow Relativity. *Nautilus*(29). Retrieved from http://nautil.us/issue/29/scaling/will-quantum-mechanics-swallow-relativity

Sartre, J.-P. (1946). *Existentialism is a Humanism*. Paris: Les Editions Nagel.

Schaffer, J. (n.d.). *The Metaphysics of Causation*. (E. N. Zalta, Ed.) Retrieved from Stanford Encyclopedia of Philosophy: https://plato.stanford.edu/archives/fall2016/entries/causation-metaphysics

Schrödinger, E. (1944). *What is Life?* Cambridge: Cambridge University Press.

Schrödinger, E. (1958). *Mind and Matter*. Cambridge: Cambridge University Press.

Sellars, W. (1962). Philosophy and the Scientific Image of Man. In *Frontiers of Science & Philosophy* (pp. 35-78). Pittsburgh: University of Pittsburgh Press.

Taylor, P. (2016, August 11). The Concept of 'Cat Face'. *London Review of Books, 38*(16), pp. 30-32. Retrieved from https://www.lrb.co.uk/v38/n16/paul-taylor/the-concept-of-cat-face

Weber, M. (1919). Politics as a Vocation. In T. Waters, & D. Waters, *Weber's Rationalism and Modern Society*. New York: Palgrave MacMillan.

Wittgenstein, L. (1953). *Philosophical Investigations*. Oxford: Basil Blackwell.

# ACKNOWLEDGEMENTS

I am grateful to everyone who has offered me comments and encouragement. I would, in particular, like to thank Michael Springer, who edited the draft, and made many invaluable suggestions for its improvement.

# INDEX TERMS

abstraction: 13-14, 28-30, 32, 35, 37-39, 41, 43-44, 49-54, 59, 61, 71, 155, 171, 236

adaptation: 9, 12, 25, 92, 97, 179, 182

agency: 108, 114, 154-155, 172

Alexander, Christopher: 9, 153

algebra: 5, 39, 140, 142, 145

algorithm: 39, 134-136, 143, 145-146, 155, 157, 160

Al-Kwarizmi: 145

analogue: 35-38, 143, 159

Aquinas, Thomas: 78, 128, 219

Aristotle: 78, 107-108

authenticity: 175, 209-210, 214-216

biological evolution: 77, 93, 136-137, 153

biology: 1, 3, 69, 92-93, 96, 99-101, 106, 135, 152, 165, 203, 221

Brand, Stewart: 6, 8-9, 22, 28, 153, 238

Brook, Rodney: 148

causal closure: 104, 106, 113, 116

cause and effect: 3, 107, 116, 118-119, 236

cellular: 18-20, 26, 72, 94

chemistry: 69, 84-85, 91, 97, 100, 102, 105, 135, 137-138, 165-166

classification: 31, 43, 45, 55, 58-60, 73, 157-159, 204, 206, 230

communication: 7, 40, 43, 144, 168-170, 202, 227

complexity: 2, 10, 91, 96, 115, 136, 153, 162-163, 177, 185-186, 189, 191, 196-197, 201, 235, 238

compositionalism: 12-13, 78

computation: 142-143, 145-146, 152, 155, 159-160

conceptual model: 35, 41, 43, 53, 55, 57-59, 118, 139, 148, 176, 199, 237

consciousness: 102-103, 131, 139, 150, 161-162, 164-165, 168-170, 174

constraint: 61, 108, 113, 116, 136-137, 170, 194-195, 199, 211-212, 235-236

copy: 30, 35-37, 186

cultural performance: 161, 168

Damasio, Antonio: 149-150, 238

Darwin, Charles: 98

decision theory: 190, 192, 196

definition: 13, 33-34, 39, 60, 75, 79, 81-82, 196

democracy: 193, 229

Dennett, Daniel: 134-135, 238

Derrida, Jaques: 41

determinism: 83, 104

domain of application: 3, 53, 57, 59-60, 62, 69, 118, 206

Dreyfus, Hubert: 147-149, 152, 238

dualism: 77, 120, 235

Duffy, Frank: 6

Dyson, Freeman: 76, 126, 238

economics: 192, 196, 203

Einstein, Albert: 65

engineering: 18, 58, 136, 146, 152, 154

epistemology: 125

essentialism: 11-12, 69-70, 77-79, 81

ethics: 14, 125, 127, 154, 175, 192-193, 203, 209, 220-221, 223-225, 229

existentialism: 127, 214, 232, 239

Feynman, Richard: 1-2, 60, 121, 238

Fodor, Jerry: 104, 238

form-giving, form-holding: 143-144, 213, 235

Godfrey-Smith, Peter: 52, 68, 75, 174, 238

Goodwin, Brian: 92, 97, 99-100, 239

Gould, Steven Jay: 125

Haugeland, John: 134

Hawking, Stephen: 3, 69, 82-83, 105, 239

Hegel, G.W.F. : 78

Heidegger, Martin: 78-80, 127-128, 148, 239

Hinton, Geoffrey: 158

Hobbes, Thomas: 23

homeostasis: 149

Hopkins, Gerard Manley: 128

humanism: 127-130, 214, 239

Hume, David: 55, 109-110

hypothesis of the real world: 102, 112, 120

idealism: 75, 102

identity: 14, 21, 23-28, 30, 44, 82, 203

incommensurability: 11, 185, 187-190, 196-197, 218

inheritance: 32, 84, 117

instrumental reasoning: 193, 208-211, 213, 215

intelligence: 14, 76, 91, 115, 130-132, 134, 137-139, 146-149, 152-155, 159, 161, 168, 173-175, 234-235

introspection: 134, 138, 161-165, 168, 171-172

# INDEX TERMS

intuition: 78, 80, 153, 238

Jaynes, Julian: 161-162, 164, 239

Kahneman, Daniel: 190, 239
Kant, Immanuel: 230
karma: 125, 225
Kierkegaard, Soren: 179, 239
Korzybski, Alfred: 36
Kripke, Saul: 80, 239
Kuhn, Thomas: 33

language: 4, 12-13, 28, 37, 40-41, 43, 47, 52-53, 56, 77, 161-162, 168-171, 173-174, 190, 199, 203
legitimacy: 175, 209-210, 214-216, 222, 226
Leibniz, G.W.: 76, 110
logic: 5, 13, 76, 81, 119, 138, 140-143, 146, 173, 231

Mach, Ernst: 75
micro-scale, macro-scale: 51, 63, 67, 71, 73-74, 76-78, 81, 85, 88, 90, 103-104, 106-107, 113-116, 120-121, 123, 132-133, 135, 137-138, 166-167, 235
materialism: 13, 73-77, 102, 104, 112, 114, 119, 129, 134, 137-138, 165

Maynard Smith, John: 92-97, 99-100, 239
mechanical: 17-18, 20, 84, 88, 99-100, 110, 114, 152-153, 155, 238
memory: 93, 116
metaphysics: 69, 78, 81, 100, 116, 125, 129, 138, 220-221, 232, 239
modular: 16-20, 26, 72, 94, 220
monism: 75, 105, 107, 113-114, 120
Morgenstern, Oskar: 190

Nagel, Thomas: 73-75, 165, 239
name: 44-48, 98, 145
naturalism: 68-69, 80, 164-165, 204, 220-221, 223
natural law: 219, 223
neural network: 155-158
neuroscience: 149, 162
numbers: 35, 49-50, 59

observable world: 12, 22, 51, 70-71, 73, 81, 113, 128, 130
observer: 16, 20, 64, 102-103, 128, 165-166, 172
order-from-disorder, order-from-order: 85, 88, 91
organic: 17, 20, 100, 115, 155

participant: 103, 165-166

243

pattern of succession: 3, 85, 88, 104, 107, 109-110, 116-117, 119, 142, 236

physics: 1, 3, 5, 22, 51-52, 60, 63, 65-67, 69, 71, 73, 75, 84-85, 87, 91-92, 97, 99-107, 113-114, 117-118, 121-123, 135, 137-138, 165-166, 238

Plato: 74, 78, 81, 108, 239

politics: 223-224, 239

Polkinghorne, John: 126

positivism: 69, 71, 82

practical reasoning: 14, 176, 185, 188-190, 196-198, 203, 209, 211, 213-214, 216, 218, 232

principle of sufficient reason: 74, 110-112, 119, 236

process: 14, 24-26, 28, 30, 32, 35, 71, 75, 77, 82, 86, 93-96, 102, 119, 128, 134, 136-138, 140, 145-146, 150, 152, 155, 158, 161-163, 166, 170, 173, 181-182, 187-189, 191, 195-197, 199-200, 207, 210-213, 215-217, 219, 224-226, 231

program: 40, 46-47, 93, 95, 97, 127, 135, 142, 145, 148-149, 155, 157

providence: 77, 125, 225

psychology: 33, 162, 238

rationality: 175, 177, 191, 196-197, 209-211, 214, 216

realism: 51, 223

reductivism: 11-12, 69-77, 100, 107, 129, 133, 165

religion: 125, 129-130, 209, 221, 238

Rosch, Eleanor: 33-34

Russell, Bertrand: 116

Sartre, Jean-Paul: 78-79, 127, 129, 214-215, 239

Schrödinger, Erwin: 84-85, 87-88, 102-103, 110, 118, 164, 239

science: 1, 11, 14, 22, 33, 37, 42, 50-51, 63, 66-70, 72-73, 75, 77, 80-81, 83, 85, 100, 102, 104-105, 107, 109, 111-113, 115, 117, 121, 123, 125-126, 129, 132-134, 137, 164-165, 221, 235-239

Scotus, John Duns: 78, 128

secularism: 125, 129-130, 225, 232

Sellars, Wilfred: 71-72, 83, 239

Shannon, Claude: 140

shearing layer: 7, 11, 22, 42, 166

significance: 18, 105, 115, 126, 145-150, 152, 154-155, 160, 169, 187, 220

Smolin, Lee: 65

Steiner, George: 128

systems thinking: 10, 119

theoretical reasoning: 198

truth: 55, 57-58, 60, 62, 104, 178, 218, 237

Turing, Alan: 131-132, 142, 145

Tversky, Amos: 190


unit of analysis: 6, 22, 46, 81

utility: 189-193, 196


value-oriented reasoning: 208-211, 226

von Neumann, John: 142, 190


Weber, Max: 208-209, 223, 239

Wittgenstein, Ludwig: 12, 33, 40, 239

words: 1, 4, 12-13, 28, 35, 40-45, 49, 53, 55, 69, 72, 108, 174, 203

www.ingramcontent.com/pod-product-compliance
Ingram Content Group UK Ltd.
Pitfield, Milton Keynes, MK11 3LW, UK
UKHW022006220326